Truly Safer

"Think Safe, Be Safe"

Handbook for Personal Safety

Tom Sotis

Truly Safer

ISBN # 978-1-300-94841-4

Imprint: Lulu.com

To the brave readers of this book:

This is dedicated to those who seek to empower themselves, who refuse to live in fear, and who understand the value of being prepared. May these pages inspire you to trust your instincts, sharpen your skills, and face the world with confidence and resilience. Your safety is your power, and your readiness is your strength. This book is for you—stay vigilant, stay safe, and keep moving forward.

Contents

Introduction

Most people go through life believing that violence is something that happens to someone else—somewhere else. They think they don't go to dangerous places, or that they're somehow immune to becoming a victim. This mindset, known as the "at-risk mentality," is a dangerous illusion that gives a false sense of security, leaving them unprepared and vulnerable. The truth is, violence doesn't discriminate by location, time, or personal circumstance. It can strike anywhere, anytime, and often to those who least expect it.

Living in a state of denial might offer temporary comfort, but it doesn't provide true security. Instead of fostering genuine self-confidence, it creates a fragile facade that can shatter in the face of real danger. The need for a deeper, more authentic sense of safety is what drives the philosophy behind Truly Safer—a transformative approach that replaces the "at-risk mentality" with the "readiness mentality."

Truly Safer is about more than just learning self-defense techniques; it's about cultivating a mindset of proactive awareness and preparedness. It empowers individuals to take control of their own safety through practical, actionable strategies that fit seamlessly into everyday life. By adopting a readiness mentality, you don't just prepare for worst-case scenarios; you enhance your overall quality of life. This approach instills a sense of personal empowerment and freedom that comes from knowing you are truly equipped to handle whatever challenges may arise.

Truly Safer coaching isn't about living in fear; it's about living freely, with the confidence that you have the skills, awareness, and protocols in place to protect yourself and your loved ones. It's about taking control of your environment, making smart decisions, and being prepared—not just physically, but mentally and emotionally. Through this book, you will learn how to shift from a passive, at-risk mentality to an active, readiness mentality that prioritizes your safety and well-being.

Imagine a life where you walk with your head held high, not out of arrogance, but out of a deep-seated assurance that you are truly safer. A life where you can enjoy your surroundings, engage fully in your activities, and live with a sense of joy and freedom that only comes from being prepared. This is the promise of Truly Safer. This is the journey we are about to embark on together.

Welcome to a new way of thinking. Welcome to a truly safer life.

Preface

Crime and violence are not abstract concepts confined to distant places or unfamiliar people; they happen in the everyday spaces where we live, work, and play. According to the U.S. Department of Justice, the vast majority of crimes occur near your residence, on the street, in parking lots and garages, in buildings, at convenience stores, gas stations, ATMs, restaurants, nightclubs, bars, on public transportation, and at places of lodging. These are the places we navigate daily, often without a second thought. Yet, they are precisely where we are most vulnerable.

Traditional safety advice often falls short because it's too generalized, relying on vague warnings to "be aware" without providing the actionable guidance needed to recognize specific dangers and respond effectively. *True safety isn't just about being aware—it's about knowing what to be aware of, when, and how to act on that knowledge. It's about context-driven solutions that address the realities of where and how confrontations are likely to occur.*

With decades of experience in personal safety and self-protection, we've developed Truly Safer coaching to bridge this critical gap. Our courses are built on the understanding that safety is situational, and the best way to be prepared is through context-driven strategies tailored to the environments where threats are most likely to arise. Whether it's the dimly lit parking lot after work, the crowded subway on your commute, or the bustling convenience store late at night, Truly Safer equips you with the skills to navigate these spaces with confidence and control.

Our approach to self-protection covers the three phases critical to personal safety: recognizing and avoiding danger, effectively managing confrontations with threatening individuals, and escaping from physical assaults. Rather than relying on one-size-fits-all advice, Truly Safer courses incorporate scenario-based activities that simulate real-world situations, providing hands-on experience in managing confrontations. These interactive strategies are not just about avoidance—they're about mastering the art of anticipation, de-escalation, and, when necessary, decisive action.

The goal of Truly Safer coaching is to make people safer in an unsafe world by focusing on the realities of where and how danger manifests. Our courses go beyond theoretical instruction to deliver practical, actionable training that empowers individuals to handle confrontations with confidence. We believe that by equipping people with context-driven skills, we can help them live more freely, with a true sense of security that comes from being prepared for whatever challenges they may face.

In this book, you will find a comprehensive guide to understanding the contexts in which threats occur and how to respond effectively. Through the principles and practices of Truly Safer, you will learn not just to survive in an unsafe world, but to thrive with the knowledge that you are truly prepared.

Welcome to a journey of empowerment, readiness, and resilience. Welcome to Truly Safer.

Part 1: Mastering Confrontations and Social Safety

De-escalating Social Conflicts

Understanding the Dynamics of Social Conflicts

Social conflicts are an inevitable part of human interaction. They can arise from simple misunderstandings, differences in opinions, or more severe issues like personal grudges or perceived slights. Understanding the dynamics of these conflicts is the first step toward effectively de-escalating them.

At their core, social conflicts often stem from unmet needs, miscommunication, or perceived threats to one's self-esteem, status, or safety. When individuals feel disrespected, ignored, or threatened, their natural response may be to defend themselves, often escalating the situation further. This reaction can manifest as verbal aggression, confrontational body language, or even physical aggression.

Another critical factor in social conflicts is the presence of ego and the desire to "win" the argument or confrontation. People are often more concerned with being right or asserting dominance rather than resolving the issue at hand. This competitive mentality can lead to stubbornness and an unwillingness to listen or compromise, further fueling the conflict.

Power imbalances also play a significant role in social conflicts. Whether in a workplace hierarchy, social setting, or public interaction, perceived differences in power can influence how conflicts unfold. Individuals in positions of perceived authority may be more assertive or dismissive, while those who feel powerless may react with defiance or submission, both of which can exacerbate the conflict.

Understanding these dynamics helps us recognize that most conflicts are not about the surface issue but are deeply rooted in emotions, perceptions, and unmet needs. By focusing on these underlying factors, we can approach conflicts with empathy and a mindset geared toward resolution rather than escalation.

Techniques for Diffusing Tense Situations

De-escalating tense situations requires a strategic approach that prioritizes calm, understanding, and communication. Here are some effective techniques to diffuse social conflicts:

Stay Calm and Composed: Your emotional state greatly influences the outcome of a conflict. If you respond with anger, frustration, or defensiveness, it's likely to escalate the situation. Instead, take a deep breath, maintain a neutral tone, and approach the situation with a calm demeanor. This can help to diffuse the tension and set a more positive tone for the interaction.

Listen Actively: One of the most effective ways to de-escalate a conflict is to listen. Active listening involves not just hearing the words but also understanding the emotions and intent behind them. It requires maintaining eye contact, nodding occasionally, and responding with empathy. By showing the other person that you genuinely care about their perspective, you can reduce their defensiveness and open the door to constructive dialogue.

Acknowledge Emotions: Often, people involved in conflicts are seeking validation for their feelings. Acknowledging emotions, even if you don't agree with the person's viewpoint, can be a powerful de-escalation tool. Phrases like "I can see that this is really upsetting for you" or "I understand that you're frustrated" can help to validate their feelings and reduce the intensity of their response.

Find Common Ground: Conflicts tend to escalate when people focus solely on their differences. Shifting the focus to commonalities can help bridge the divide. Identifying shared goals, values, or experiences can help both parties feel more connected and less adversarial. This can pave the way for more collaborative problem-solving.

Use "I" Statements: Instead of accusing or blaming the other person, frame your concerns using "I" statements. For example, say "I feel concerned when…" rather than "You always…". This approach focuses on your perspective and feelings rather than assigning blame, which can reduce defensiveness and encourage a more open dialogue.

Set Boundaries: While de-escalation is about diffusing tension, it's also important to set clear boundaries if the other person's behavior becomes abusive or unacceptable. Calmly and firmly state what behavior is not acceptable and what the consequences will be if it continues. This shows that while you're willing to engage in resolving the conflict, you won't tolerate disrespect or aggression.

Offer Solutions or Compromises: Moving towards resolution involves finding a way forward that meets the needs of both parties. Offer solutions or compromises that address the core issues of the conflict. Be willing to give a little and ask the other person to do the same. This collaborative approach can help shift the dynamic from confrontation to cooperation.

Take a Break if Needed: Sometimes, conflicts can become too heated to resolve in the moment. If you feel that emotions are running too high, suggest taking a break and revisiting the conversation after a cooling-off period. This pause allows both parties to reflect, calm down, and approach the issue with a clearer mind.

Using Body Language and Verbal Skills to Calm Confrontations

Body language and verbal communication play crucial roles in how conflicts unfold and can be powerful tools for de-escalation. Here's how to use them effectively:

Non-Threatening Body Language: Your body language should convey openness and calmness. Avoid crossing your arms, clenching your fists, or pointing fingers, as these can be perceived as aggressive or confrontational. Instead, maintain an open posture, keep your hands visible, and use gentle gestures to emphasize your points.

Maintain Eye Contact: Eye contact shows that you're engaged and taking the other person seriously. However, be mindful of not staring too intensely, as this can be seen as a challenge. Aim for soft, steady eye contact that communicates attentiveness and respect.

Mind Your Tone and Pace: The tone and pace of your speech can significantly impact the interaction. Speak in a calm, steady voice, and avoid raising your pitch, which can be perceived as agitation or aggression. Slower speech can also help calm the situation, as it encourages a more thoughtful and less reactive exchange.

Mirror and Match: Subtly mirroring the other person's body language can create a sense of rapport and understanding. For example, if they are sitting, you might sit as well. If they are speaking softly, match your volume to theirs. This technique can make the other person feel more at ease and open to dialogue.

Use Positive Reinforcement: Encourage constructive behavior by acknowledging positive actions or words during the conflict. For example, if the other person begins to speak more calmly, you might say, "I appreciate that you're sharing your thoughts calmly." Positive reinforcement can help guide the conversation towards a more productive and peaceful resolution.

Stay Focused on the Issue, Not the Person: It's easy for conflicts to become personal attacks. Redirect the focus to the issue at hand rather than allowing it to become a critique of the individual. For instance, instead of saying, "You're always causing problems," try, "Let's figure out how we can solve this issue together." This approach keeps the conversation goal-oriented and less emotionally charged.

De-escalating social conflicts is a skill that requires patience, empathy, and strategic communication. By understanding the dynamics of conflicts and employing these techniques, you can transform potentially volatile situations into opportunities for constructive dialogue and resolution. With practice, these skills not only make you more adept at handling conflicts but also contribute to building stronger, more positive relationships in all areas of your life.

Managing Adult Challengers

Identifying Workplace and Public Bullies

While bullying is often associated with schoolyard antics, it doesn't disappear in adulthood. Instead, it can manifest in the workplace, public spaces, and social settings. Adult bullies can be colleagues, supervisors, acquaintances, or strangers who use intimidation, manipulation, or harassment to assert control or undermine others. Recognizing these individuals early on is crucial to managing their behavior and protecting your mental and emotional well-being.

Adult bullies in the workplace may use various tactics to exert power, such as belittling comments, exclusion from important conversations or decisions, unwarranted criticism, or spreading rumors. They often target individuals they perceive as threats, or those they consider vulnerable due to lower status or perceived differences. Their actions can create a toxic work environment, leading to stress, reduced productivity, and even job dissatisfaction or loss.

In public or social settings, adult bullies may be those who use aggressive behavior to dominate conversations, make others feel uncomfortable, or publicly demean people to boost their own ego. They thrive on creating a power imbalance, often testing boundaries to see how much they can get away with. Recognizing these behaviors—such as someone repeatedly interrupting, making sarcastic or cutting remarks, or physically invading your space—is the first step in addressing the problem.

Understanding the motivations behind adult bullying can also help in dealing with these individuals. Many adult bullies act out of insecurity, a desire for control, or unresolved personal issues. By identifying these patterns, you can approach interactions with a strategic mindset, rather than reacting emotionally or feeling helpless.

Verbal Judo: Strategies for Standing Your Ground Without Escalation

Once you've identified a bully, the next step is learning how to manage interactions in a way that protects your dignity and safety without escalating the conflict. This is where verbal judo—a set of communication techniques designed to deflect aggression and maintain control of the conversation—comes into play. Verbal judo focuses on redirecting hostility, disarming the aggressor, and standing your ground calmly and confidently.

The Power of Empathy: One of the foundational principles of verbal judo is empathy. By acknowledging the other person's feelings and showing that you understand their perspective, you can often diffuse hostility and create an opening for constructive dialogue. Phrases like, "I can see that you're upset," or "I understand why this is important to you," can help to lower the emotional temperature of the conversation and demonstrate that you're willing to listen.

Deflecting Aggression: When confronted with aggressive or hostile behavior, direct confrontation can often escalate the situation. Instead, verbal judo teaches the art of deflection—redirecting the conversation away from a negative path and onto a more neutral or positive track. This can involve changing the subject, asking a question to redirect the aggressor's focus, or using humor to lighten the mood. For example, if someone is criticizing you unfairly, you might say, "That's an interesting perspective. What do you suggest as a solution?" This approach takes the wind out of the aggressor's sails and shifts the focus from attack to problem-solving.

The "Broken Record" Technique: This strategy involves calmly and consistently repeating your position or request, regardless of the aggressor's attempts to sidetrack or provoke you. By sticking to your message without getting drawn into their emotional bait, you maintain control of the interaction. For example, if a bully is pushing you to take on an unreasonable task at work, you might calmly repeat, "I'm happy to help with that once I've completed my current priorities," no matter how many times they try to push back.

Assertive Body Language: Verbal judo isn't just about what you say—how you present yourself is equally important. Maintain a confident posture, make eye contact, and keep your tone even and controlled. These nonverbal cues reinforce your verbal message and convey that you are not intimidated or rattled, even if the bully attempts to provoke you.

Disarming with Respect: Showing respect to someone who is being disrespectful may seem counterintuitive, but it can be a powerful tactic. By treating the aggressor with more respect than they are showing you, you effectively disarm their hostility and often leave them with little room to continue their negative behavior without looking unreasonable. Phrases like "I respect your opinion," or "Thank you for sharing your thoughts," can neutralize aggression by taking away the aggressor's perceived justification for their actions.

Reframing the Conversation: Another key strategy in verbal judo is reframing the conversation to focus on solutions rather than problems. For example, if someone is fixated on criticizing your work, you might say, "I appreciate your feedback. Let's focus on what we can do to improve this going forward." This shifts the conversation from blame to constructive action, which can defuse tension and guide the interaction toward a positive outcome.

Setting Boundaries and Protecting Your Personal Space

Setting boundaries is essential for managing adult challengers. Boundaries communicate your limits and establish clear lines that others should not cross. They protect your personal space, time, and emotional well-being from those who may seek to exploit or manipulate you.

Be Clear and Direct: When setting boundaries, clarity is key. Clearly communicate what is acceptable and what is not, without ambiguity. For example, if a colleague frequently interrupts you during meetings, a clear boundary might be, "I would appreciate it if you could let me finish my thoughts before jumping in." Being direct doesn't mean being confrontational; it's about asserting your needs calmly and respectfully.

Use "I" Statements: Frame your boundaries using "I" statements to make them about your needs rather than blaming the other person. This approach reduces defensiveness and makes it clear that you are taking responsibility for your own comfort and safety. For instance, "I feel uncomfortable when discussions get personal, and I prefer to keep things professional."

Consistency is Crucial: Once you've set a boundary, it's important to consistently enforce it. Inconsistency sends mixed messages and can encourage further boundary violations. If someone repeatedly crosses your boundaries despite your requests, reiterate your stance firmly and consider escalating the matter if necessary, such as involving HR in a workplace setting.

Recognize and Respect Your Limits: Part of setting boundaries is recognizing your own limits and respecting them. This means not overextending yourself or compromising your values to appease others. It's okay to say no to additional tasks when you're already at capacity, or to remove yourself from a conversation that is becoming too heated or personal.

Practice Self-Protection Strategies: Protecting your personal space also involves physical boundaries. If someone invades your personal space, step back to reassert your physical boundary. In public or social settings, maintain a comfortable distance from aggressive individuals and position yourself in a way that allows for a clear exit if needed.

Don't Be Afraid to Disengage: If a situation becomes too confrontational or your boundaries are not being respected, it's okay to disengage. Politely excuse yourself from the conversation or leave the environment if possible. Your safety and peace of mind are more important than winning an argument or standing your ground in a hostile setting.

Managing adult challengers is about maintaining your composure, protecting your personal space, and using strategic communication to stand your ground without escalating the conflict. By recognizing the signs of bullying, employing verbal judo techniques, and setting clear boundaries, you can navigate challenging interactions with confidence and assertiveness. These skills not only help you handle difficult individuals effectively but also contribute to a healthier, more respectful environment in both your personal and professional life.

Confronting Criminals

Recognizing the Signs of Potential Threats

Confronting criminals is a daunting scenario that many of us hope never to face. However, preparing for such encounters is essential to maintaining personal safety. The first step in effectively managing these situations is recognizing the signs of potential threats. Criminals often exhibit certain behaviors and patterns that can serve as warning signals, allowing you to take preventive actions before a situation escalates.

One of the most crucial aspects of threat recognition is situational awareness. This involves being fully aware of your surroundings, noting anything unusual or out of place, and paying attention to the behavior of those around you. Common signs of potential threats include individuals who are loitering in an area without a clear purpose, showing an unusual interest in your movements, or appearing overly focused on their environment as if they're scoping out potential targets. Individuals who avoid eye contact or, conversely, stare intensely can also be indicators of suspicious intent.

Pre-assault cues are another set of signals that can indicate imminent danger. These cues can include aggressive body language such as clenched fists, pacing, rapid breathing, or repeatedly glancing at your belongings or their own hands. A person who is trying to hide their face, such as with a hood or sunglasses in an inappropriate setting, may also be preparing for criminal activity. Trust your instincts; if something feels off, it probably is. Our intuition often picks up on subtle cues that our conscious mind might overlook.

It's also important to be aware of environmental factors that increase the likelihood of encountering criminals. High-risk locations include isolated parking lots, dimly lit alleys, ATM kiosks, and quiet public transportation areas late at night. Avoiding these places or, at the very least, being extra vigilant when navigating them, can significantly reduce your risk.

By understanding and recognizing the signs of potential threats, you can take preemptive measures such as changing your route, moving to a more populated area, or preparing to defend yourself if necessary. Proactive awareness is your first line of defense in confronting criminals.

What to Say and Do When Confronted by a Mugger or Assailant

If you find yourself face-to-face with a criminal, such as a mugger or assailant, your actions in those critical first moments can determine the outcome of the encounter. The primary objective is always to de-escalate the situation and minimize the risk of harm to yourself. Here's what to say and do when confronted:

Remain Calm and Composed: Although it's natural to feel fear and anxiety, showing visible panic can escalate the aggressor's behavior. Take deep breaths and focus on staying as calm as possible. A calm demeanor not only helps you think more clearly but can also have a calming effect on the assailant.

Comply and De-escalate: In situations like muggings, where the aggressor's primary motive is usually to take your valuables, compliance is often the safest option. Hand over your wallet, phone, or whatever is demanded without argument. Your possessions can be replaced; your safety cannot. Use non-threatening body language—keep your hands visible, avoid sudden movements, and maintain a submissive posture that shows you are not a threat.

Use Simple and Clear Language: When confronted, it's crucial to communicate clearly and concisely. Use phrases that show compliance and a willingness to cooperate, such as "Okay, I'm giving you what you want," or "I'm doing what you say." Avoid aggressive or confrontational language, as it can provoke further aggression.

Keep Your Distance: If possible, maintain a safe distance between yourself and the assailant. This not only gives you more reaction time but also reduces the likelihood of physical contact. If the assailant steps closer, take a small step back to maintain that space without making it appear that you're trying to flee, which could trigger a chase.

Avoid Eye Contact but Stay Aware: Direct eye contact can be perceived as a challenge or threat, but completely looking away can make you seem overly submissive. Aim to glance occasionally without staring, staying aware of the assailant's movements and any potential escape routes.

Do Not Argue or Resist: Resisting, arguing, or trying to negotiate with a criminal who is clearly intent on taking your belongings can quickly escalate the situation to violence. The goal is to defuse tension, not to win an argument or protect your possessions. If the situation allows, make slow, deliberate movements and follow the assailant's instructions as calmly as possible.

Create Opportunities to Escape: While complying, look for potential opportunities to safely distance yourself from the situation. This might include moving to a more crowded area, positioning yourself near an exit, or using the environment to create a barrier between you and the assailant. If you see an opening to safely flee, do so decisively and without hesitation.

Be Ready to Act if the Threat Escalates: If the assailant shows intent to harm you physically despite your compliance, you may need to defend yourself. Be prepared to use any means available, such as a personal safety device (pepper spray, personal alarm), or to physically defend yourself if trained and confident in doing so. The decision to fight back is a personal one and should be made based on the severity of the threat and your ability to effectively protect yourself.

Techniques for Staying Calm and Making Smart Decisions Under Pressure

Staying calm under pressure is a critical skill when facing a confrontation with a criminal. Your ability to think clearly and make smart decisions can be the difference between a safe outcome and a dangerous escalation.

Here are techniques to help you maintain composure and make sound decisions when confronted:

Control Your Breathing: When faced with a threatening situation, your body's natural response is the fight-or-flight reaction, which can cause rapid breathing, increased heart rate, and heightened anxiety. Controlling your breathing is one of the quickest ways to calm your body and mind. Practice taking slow, deep breaths—inhale through your nose for a count of four, hold for four, and exhale through your mouth for four. This simple exercise can help reduce panic and bring your focus back to the present moment.

Focus on the Task at Hand: In high-stress situations, your mind may race with "what if" scenarios and worst-case outcomes. Redirect your focus to the immediate task at hand—complying with the assailant's demands, looking for a safe escape route, or preparing to defend yourself. By narrowing your attention to actionable steps, you can prevent your thoughts from spiraling and maintain a sense of control.

Use Visualization Techniques: Visualizing a safe outcome can help manage fear and anxiety. Picture yourself complying smoothly and walking away unharmed. Visualization can help reinforce positive actions and reduce panic, guiding you toward decisions that prioritize your safety.

Practice Mindfulness: Mindfulness involves staying fully present in the moment without judgment. In a confrontation, this means focusing on what you see, hear, and feel right now, rather than becoming overwhelmed by fear of what might happen next. Mindfulness can help ground you, keeping you alert and ready to respond appropriately to any changes in the situation.

Prepare Mentally for Confrontations: Mental preparation is key to staying calm under pressure. Regularly practicing scenarios in your mind, such as how you would react if confronted by a mugger, can help condition your response. This rehearsal builds mental resilience and makes it easier to recall effective strategies when faced with real threats.

Trust Your Instincts: Your intuition is a powerful tool in assessing danger. If something doesn't feel right, trust that feeling and take immediate action to protect yourself. Whether it's fleeing the scene, complying with demands, or calling for help, trusting your gut can guide you toward the safest course of action.

Debrief and Learn from Each Experience: If you have been confronted by a criminal, take time afterward to debrief the experience. What went well? What could you have done differently? Reflecting on these moments, even if they were not perfect, can help you prepare better for future encounters and build confidence in your ability to handle such situations.

Confronting criminals is an unnerving experience, but by recognizing potential threats, knowing what to say and do, and employing techniques to stay calm, you can navigate these dangerous situations with a greater sense of control and safety. Remember, the ultimate goal is to protect yourself and those around you by making smart, proactive decisions under pressure.

Part 2: Safety Protocols for Everyday Environments

Residential Safety

Ensuring the safety of your home and its occupants is a fundamental priority for many individuals and families. Residential safety encompasses a range of strategies, from assessing vulnerabilities within the home to creating robust layers of security and staying vigilant to suspicious activities in the neighborhood. By taking a comprehensive approach, you can significantly reduce the risk of break-ins, theft, or other threats. Let's explore how to enhance residential safety through three critical steps: assessing your home's vulnerability, creating layers of security, and recognizing suspicious behavior in your neighborhood.

Assessing Your Home's Vulnerability

The first step in enhancing residential safety is to assess your home's vulnerability to potential threats. This involves evaluating physical aspects of the property, understanding the habits of the household members, and considering the location of the residence. Conducting a thorough vulnerability assessment helps identify weak points that could be exploited by intruders.

Exterior Assessment: Start by examining the exterior of your home. Look for areas that could provide easy access to an intruder, such as low-hanging tree branches near windows, unlocked gates, or poor lighting. Check for damaged or unlocked windows, doors that could be easily forced open, and any areas that are hidden from public view where someone could approach unnoticed. Pay attention to the condition of fences, walls, and other barriers that could be used to climb over into your property.

Entry Points: Windows and doors are the most common entry points for burglars. Check the strength and quality of locks and consider upgrading to more secure options such as deadbolts, smart locks, or window bars. Ensure that sliding doors have secure locking mechanisms and add a bar or rod in the track to prevent them from being forced open.

Interior Assessment: Evaluate how easy it would be for someone to gain entry and move around inside your home. Are there valuables visible from windows? Do you leave doors unlocked when you're at home? Consider the layout of your home and identify areas that might provide concealment for an intruder.

Technology and Monitoring: Assess the technology you have in place, such as security cameras, alarms, and motion detectors. Are these systems up-to-date and functioning properly? Do they cover all vulnerable areas? An outdated or malfunctioning system can be a weak link in your home's security.

Lifestyle Habits: Consider the habits of those living in the home. Do you often leave doors or windows unlocked? Are packages left unattended outside? Does anyone regularly post on social media about vacations or extended absences? These behaviors can increase the risk of your home being targeted.

Creating Layers of Security at Home

Once you have assessed the vulnerabilities of your home, the next step is to create multiple layers of security. This approach makes it more difficult for potential intruders to successfully target your home, as they must bypass several obstacles.

Perimeter Security: Start by securing the perimeter of your property. This can include installing sturdy fences, gates, and walls, as well as using thorny bushes or other natural barriers. Good lighting is essential; install motion-activated lights to illuminate dark areas and deter intruders. Security signs, such as those indicating that the property is under surveillance or protected by a guard dog, can also be effective deterrents.

Entry Point Reinforcement: Strengthen all entry points to your home. Invest in high-quality locks for doors and windows and consider smart locks that can be controlled remotely. Use security film on windows to make them more resistant to breaking and install peepholes or doorbell cameras so you can see who is at your door before opening it.

Interior Security Measures: Inside the home, consider using alarms and sensors that detect movement or break-ins. Install a security system that alerts you or a monitoring service if an intrusion is detected. Keep valuable items in a safe that is securely bolted down and ensure that important documents and valuables are not easily accessible.

Technology Integration: Modern technology provides numerous options for enhancing residential safety. Smart home systems allow you to control lighting, locks, and cameras from your smartphone. Set up cameras to monitor key areas of your home and use apps to receive real-time alerts if suspicious activity is detected. Doorbell cameras and intercoms also provide an additional layer of security, allowing you to communicate with visitors without opening the door.

Behavioral Adjustments: Some of the most effective security measures involve changes in behavior. Always lock doors and windows, even when you are at home. Be mindful of what you post on social media and avoid sharing details about your whereabouts or vacations. If you are expecting deliveries, try to schedule them for times when you will be home, or use secure delivery options that require a signature.

Recognizing Suspicious Behavior in Your Neighborhood

Being vigilant about suspicious activity in your neighborhood is another critical aspect of residential safety. Criminals often scout neighborhoods before attempting a break-in, and recognizing signs of suspicious behavior can help prevent crimes before they occur.

Know Your Neighbors: Building a rapport with your neighbors creates a network of people who can look out for each other. Get to know the regular patterns of people in your neighborhood, including who lives where and what cars they drive. This familiarity makes it easier to spot something out of the ordinary.

Unfamiliar Vehicles or People: Be alert to vehicles that are unfamiliar or seem out of place, especially if they are parked for long periods or repeatedly seen driving slowly through the area. Similarly, watch for unfamiliar people who are loitering, walking around aimlessly, or appearing to take an unusual interest in homes.

Scouting Behavior: Criminals often engage in scouting behavior, such as looking into windows, checking door handles, or taking photos of properties. If you observe someone doing this, do not confront them directly but make a note of their description and report it to the police or neighborhood watch.

Door-to-Door Scams: Be cautious of individuals going door-to-door with unsolicited offers for home repairs, landscaping, or other services, especially if they seem pushy or are unable to provide identification. These could be scams or attempts to gain access to your home for reconnaissance.

Unusual Activity: Pay attention to unusual activity, such as hearing sounds of breaking glass, seeing people running or acting furtively, or noticing doors or windows open when they should not be. If something seems suspicious, trust your instincts and report it to the authorities.

By taking a proactive approach to assessing your home's vulnerabilities, creating layers of security, and recognizing suspicious behavior, you can significantly enhance the safety of your residence. A secure home not only protects your belongings but also provides peace of mind for you and your family.

Safer on the Street

Navigating the streets safely requires more than just being aware of your surroundings; it involves adopting a mindset that prioritizes your personal security at all times. Whether walking through familiar neighborhoods or unfamiliar urban environments, the ability to avoid danger, identify potential threats, and maintain a low profile is essential. This guide covers street-smart strategies for staying safe, recognizing and steering clear of potential dangers, and developing situational awareness to help you navigate the streets with confidence.

Street-Smart Strategies for Avoiding Danger

Being street-smart means having practical knowledge and skills that allow you to handle challenging situations effectively. These strategies are not about living in fear but about being prepared and proactive in keeping yourself safe.

Plan Your Route: One of the most effective ways to avoid danger is to plan your route in advance. Choose well-lit, busy streets over dark alleys or deserted shortcuts. Familiarize yourself with the area, noting the locations of police stations, businesses that are open late, and other safe places where you can seek help if needed. Use navigation apps that provide real-time information about traffic, crowds, and any reported incidents.

Blend In: Standing out in a crowd can make you a target, especially if you appear unfamiliar with your surroundings. Dress inconspicuously and avoid wearing flashy jewelry or expensive accessories that might attract unwanted attention. Walk with confidence, even if you are unsure of your exact location; projecting an air of confidence can deter potential threats.

Trust Your Instincts: Your instincts are often your first line of defense. If something feels off or if a situation seems unsafe, trust your gut and take action to remove yourself from the area. This might mean crossing the street, ducking into a store, or changing your route altogether. It's better to be overly cautious than to dismiss a potential threat.

Keep Your Hands Free: To react quickly in an emergency, keep your hands as free as possible. Avoid walking while engrossed in your phone or carrying too many items. If you need to carry bags, consider using a backpack to keep your hands available. This not only allows you to defend yourself if necessary but also makes you less vulnerable to theft.

Stay Sober and Alert: Being under the influence of alcohol or drugs impairs your judgment and reaction time, making you an easier target. If you plan to drink, do so in moderation and stay with a trusted group. Always have a plan for getting home safely, such as arranging a designated driver or using a trusted rideshare service.

Use Technology Wisely: While your phone can be a lifeline in emergencies, it can also be a distraction. Use technology wisely by setting your destination before leaving and keeping your phone accessible but not visible. Share your location with a trusted friend or family member, especially if you are traveling alone or in unfamiliar areas.

How to Identify and Steer Clear of Potential Threats

Recognizing potential threats before they escalate is crucial for personal safety. Criminals often look for easy targets, so being able to identify and avoid risky situations can make a significant difference.

Body Language and Behavior: Pay attention to the body language and behavior of people around you. Signs of potential threats include individuals who are overly interested in your movements, those who are loitering without a clear purpose, or anyone who appears to be following you. People who are scanning the area frequently or trying to hide their face might also be up to no good.

Avoid Isolated Areas: Stay away from isolated or poorly lit areas, such as empty parking lots, stairwells, or alleyways. These locations provide cover for would-be attackers and reduce your chances of finding help quickly. Stick to areas with good visibility and plenty of foot traffic.

Be Cautious with Strangers: While most people you encounter on the street are harmless, be wary of strangers who approach you with unsolicited requests or offers. Common tactics include asking for directions, money, or assistance with a broken-down vehicle. Keep a safe distance and be polite but firm in declining any requests that make you uncomfortable.

Avoid Predictable Patterns: Criminals often look for predictable patterns, such as walking the same route every day or leaving at the same time. If possible, vary your routines to make it harder for someone to anticipate your movements. This is especially important if you feel you are being watched or followed.

Recognize and Avoid Scams: Scams on the street can range from fake charity collections to overly friendly individuals trying to distract you while an accomplice steals from you. Be skeptical of anyone who tries to engage you in unexpected conversation or asks for money. If a situation doesn't seem right, politely excuse yourself and leave the area.

Watch for Warning Signs: Warning signs of potential threats include unusual noises, such as breaking glass, shouting, or sudden silence in a normally noisy area. If you notice these signs, take them seriously and remove yourself from the situation. Similarly, if you see someone acting erratically or aggressively, keep your distance and seek safety.

Developing Situational Awareness and Maintaining a Low Profile

Situational awareness is the practice of being mindful of your surroundings and understanding what is happening around you at all times. This skill can help you identify potential dangers early and take action to avoid them.

Observe Your Environment: Make it a habit to regularly scan your surroundings. Take note of exits, potential hazards, and the people around you. This doesn't mean being paranoid but rather staying alert and aware. Pay attention to changes in the environment, such as someone new entering your space or an unfamiliar car parked nearby.

Stay Off Your Phone: One of the biggest distractions on the street is your phone. While it's important to stay connected, try to keep phone use to a minimum when walking. If you need to make a call or send a message, find a safe place to stop rather than walking and using your phone simultaneously.

Maintain a Low Profile: Being discreet about your actions and belongings can help you avoid attracting attention. Keep your valuables, such as phones, wallets, and jewelry, out of sight. If you need to access something valuable, do so discreetly and in a secure location.

Use Reflection to Your Advantage: You can use reflections in windows or mirrors to check if someone is following you without turning around. This can help you maintain awareness of your surroundings while appearing less obvious in your actions.

Practice Defensive Walking: Walk facing traffic, when possible, as this makes it harder for someone to approach you from behind in a vehicle. Keep a healthy distance from buildings, especially doorways or alley entrances where someone could hide. Stay in the middle of the sidewalk, where you have the most room to maneuver if needed.

Create Personal Boundaries: If someone gets too close for comfort, don't hesitate to assert your personal space.

A firm "No" or "Please keep your distance" can be enough to deter someone from encroaching on your space. Use your body language to communicate confidence, such as standing tall and making eye contact.

Have an Exit Strategy: Always have a plan for how you will leave a situation if it becomes unsafe. This could mean knowing the nearest exit in a building, identifying a safe place to go if you feel threatened, or having a quick response ready if someone tries to engage you. Practice thinking one step ahead, so you're not caught off guard.

By adopting these street-smart strategies, honing your ability to identify threats, and developing strong situational awareness, you can significantly increase your safety on the streets. Remember, the goal is not to be paranoid but to be prepared and proactive in protecting yourself from potential dangers.

Parking & Vehicle Safety

Ensuring your safety and the security of your vehicle when parking or in transit is a critical aspect of personal security. Whether you're navigating parking lots, garages, or gas stations, or dealing with a vehicle breakdown, understanding best practices can help you avoid potential dangers. This guide explores the essential strategies for staying safe in parking lots, garages, and gas stations, protocols to follow if your vehicle breaks down, and tips for staying alert and avoiding distractions in vulnerable spaces.

Best Practices for Parking Lots, Garages, and Gas Stations

Parking lots, garages, and gas stations are common locations where people can be vulnerable to theft, assault, or accidents. By adopting the following best practices, you can minimize your risk and increase your safety in these spaces.

Choose Safe Parking Spots: Whenever possible, park in well-lit areas that are close to entrances or exits and avoid isolated spots. Look for parking spaces that have a clear view of your surroundings and that are visible to other people. Avoid parking near large vehicles, bushes, or structures that could provide cover for someone attempting to hide.

Be Mindful of Your Surroundings: Before parking, take a moment to observe the area. Look for anything or anyone that seems out of place or suspicious. If something feels off, trust your instincts and choose a different location.

When exiting or approaching your vehicle, stay alert and keep your head up, scanning the environment rather than being distracted by your phone.

Secure Your Vehicle: Always lock your vehicle, even if you're only stepping away for a brief moment. Ensure all windows are fully closed and valuables are hidden from sight, as visible items can tempt thieves. If you have a car alarm, use it to add an extra layer of security.

Stay Aware in Garages: Parking garages can be particularly vulnerable spaces due to their enclosed and often poorly lit nature. Use stairs instead of elevators when possible, as stairwells are more open and visible. Avoid walking directly between parked cars and choose routes that keep you in more open areas with better visibility.

Safety at Gas Stations: When fueling up, stay with your vehicle and remain aware of your surroundings. Avoid leaving your vehicle unlocked or your keys in the ignition, even if you're standing right next to it. If you need to go inside the store, take your keys with you and lock your car. Be cautious of people approaching you for money or assistance; if you feel uncomfortable, go inside the store or remain in your locked vehicle.

Watch for Common Scams: Be aware of common scams in these areas, such as people approaching you with fake emergencies, requests for money, or offers to clean your windshield unsolicited. These can be distractions intended to steal from you or your vehicle.

Politely decline and keep your distance if something doesn't seem right.

Walk With Confidence: Walking with purpose and confidence can deter potential threats. Keep your keys in your hand as you approach your car; they can be used as a weapon if necessary and reduce the time it takes to enter your vehicle. Before getting in, take a quick look inside and around your car to ensure no one is hiding nearby.

Vehicle Breakdown Safety Protocols

Breaking down on the road can be a stressful and potentially dangerous situation. Knowing the proper safety protocols can help you stay safe until help arrives.

Move to a Safe Location: If your vehicle starts to malfunction, try to move to the right shoulder of the road or into a parking lot if possible. Aim for a location that is away from traffic and has good visibility. If you're unable to move your car, turn on your hazard lights immediately to alert other drivers.

Make Your Vehicle Visible: Use hazard lights, flares, or reflective triangles to make your vehicle more visible to other drivers, especially at night or in poor weather conditions. Place warning devices at least 100 feet behind your car to give other drivers plenty of notice.

Stay Inside Your Vehicle: In most cases, it's safer to stay inside your vehicle with the doors locked and seatbelt fastened, especially if you are on a busy road or highway. If you must exit the vehicle, do so on the side away from traffic and stay as far from the roadway as possible. Avoid standing in front of or behind your vehicle to reduce the risk of being hit if another driver loses control.

Call for Assistance: Use your phone to call for roadside assistance, a tow truck, or the police if you're in an unsafe area. Keep emergency contact numbers and information about your roadside assistance plan readily accessible. If you don't have a phone or service, look for emergency call boxes along highways.

Be Cautious of Strangers Offering Help: While most people may genuinely want to assist, it's important to be cautious. If someone stops to help, remain in your vehicle and lower your window only slightly to communicate. Politely inform them that help is on the way. Avoid accepting rides from strangers and wait for professional assistance.

Use Emergency Supplies: Keep an emergency kit in your car that includes items like a flashlight, first aid kit, water, blankets, and basic tools. A charged portable phone charger is also essential for maintaining communication if your phone battery runs low.

Staying Alert and Avoiding Distractions in Vulnerable Spaces

Staying alert and avoiding distractions is crucial when you are in vulnerable spaces such as parking lots, garages, and gas stations. Distractions can make you an easy target for opportunistic crimes. Here are strategies to help you stay vigilant.

Minimize Phone Use: While your phone is a valuable tool for communication and navigation, it can also be a major distraction. Try to complete calls or texts before you enter these spaces, and keep your phone in your pocket or bag until you are safely inside your vehicle. If you need to use your phone, do so while stationary and in a safe location.

Listen to Your Environment: Instead of wearing headphones or earbuds, listen to your surroundings. This allows you to hear approaching footsteps, voices, or other sounds that might indicate potential danger. If you must use headphones, keep the volume low or use only one earbud so you remain partially aware.

Keep Personal Items Secure: Carry personal items like bags, purses, or backpacks close to your body and zipped up. This reduces the likelihood of being targeted by pickpockets or snatch-and-grab thieves. Avoid carrying too many bags at once, as this can hinder your movement and make you less aware of your surroundings.

Avoid Routine Behavior: Criminals often look for predictable patterns, so try to vary your parking locations, the times you visit certain places, and your general routines. This makes it harder for someone to anticipate your movements and reduces the risk of being targeted.

Use Reflection to Stay Aware: Utilize reflections in windows, car mirrors, or other surfaces to discreetly observe your surroundings. This allows you to check behind you without turning around fully, which can be useful if you suspect someone might be following you.

Practice Defensive Parking: When possible, park in a way that allows you to drive forward rather than backing out, as this provides a quicker and safer departure. Avoid parking next to vans or large vehicles that obstruct your view or could conceal someone waiting to ambush you.

7. Have Your Keys Ready: Before leaving a building or store, have your car keys ready in your hand. This reduces the time you spend at your car and makes it easier to enter quickly. Avoid fumbling for your keys at your vehicle, which leaves you vulnerable to attack or theft.

By adhering to these best practices for parking and vehicle safety, you can significantly reduce the risk of becoming a victim in these vulnerable spaces. Staying alert, prepared, and mindful of your environment not only enhances your personal safety but also boosts your confidence when navigating public spaces.

Safer in Buildings

Ensuring your safety inside buildings involves more than just being aware of your surroundings; it requires specific strategies to navigate common spaces such as restrooms, stairwells, elevators, and hallways. Enclosed environments can present unique risks, from petty crimes to emergency situations, making it crucial to recognize red flags and know how to use emergency exits and escape routes effectively. This guide provides practical advice on how to stay safe in various building spaces, how to identify potential dangers, and how to prepare for emergencies.

Navigating Restrooms, Stairwells, Elevators, and Hallways Safely

Navigating common areas in buildings safely involves being alert and proactive. Restrooms, stairwells, elevators, and hallways are often enclosed and less visible to others, which can make them hotspots for potential threats. Here's how to stay safe in these spaces:

1. Restrooms: Public restrooms are often isolated from main traffic areas, making them potential spots for confrontations or theft.

Enter with Awareness: Before entering, take a moment to observe the surroundings. If the restroom is in a secluded area or if you notice anyone lingering outside who makes you uncomfortable, consider finding another restroom.

Choose the Right Stall: Select a stall that is closest to the entrance or the one that allows you to see if anyone else enters. If possible, avoid stalls that are out of view or too deep into the restroom.

Stay Alert: While using the restroom, keep an ear out for unusual sounds, such as footsteps approaching your stall or someone trying to open doors. If something feels off, prepare to leave quickly.

Avoid Distractions: Refrain from using your phone or other distractions while in a restroom. Staying focused on your surroundings will help you detect any unusual activity early.

2. Stairwells: Stairwells are often isolated and offer limited visibility, making them places where incidents can occur unnoticed.

Use During High Traffic Times: If possible, use stairwells during busy times when more people are around. This reduces the likelihood of encountering someone with ill intentions.

Stay Near Exits: If you need to use a stairwell, stay near exits and avoid descending or ascending too far into secluded areas. Enter or exit on floors with high visibility and traffic.

Avoid Headphones: While using stairwells, avoid wearing headphones or being otherwise distracted. Listen for footsteps, voices, or other sounds that might indicate someone is nearby.

Keep Moving: If you feel uneasy, keep moving and exit as soon as possible. Avoid stopping or lingering, especially in areas with poor lighting.

3. Elevators: Elevators can be confined spaces where you are in close proximity to strangers, making them potentially uncomfortable or risky.

Stand Near Controls: When entering an elevator, position yourself near the control panel so you can quickly press buttons in an emergency. If someone makes you uncomfortable, press the next floor's button and exit as soon as possible.

Let Others Exit First: Allow others to exit before you enter, giving you a clear view of who is inside. If you feel uneasy about someone in the elevator, wait for the next one.

Avoid Crowded Elevators: If an elevator is overcrowded, consider waiting for the next one. Crowded elevators not only pose a fire hazard but also make it easier for pickpockets or others with ill intent to act without being noticed.

Exit on Public Floors: If you feel threatened, exit on a floor with high visibility, such as the lobby or a floor with businesses and people.

4. Hallways: Hallways are transitional spaces that can also pose risks, particularly if they are long, poorly lit, or rarely used.

Stay to the Sides: Walk near the walls rather than down the center of a hallway. This reduces the likelihood of being surprised from behind or from around a corner.

Listen and Observe: Pay attention to your environment by listening for footsteps, doors opening, or voices. If you sense someone following you, be prepared to alter your route or enter a nearby occupied space.

Avoid Empty or Poorly Lit Areas: Choose hallways that are well-lit and frequently used. If you must use a deserted hallway, move quickly and confidently to your destination.

Recognizing Red Flags in Enclosed Spaces

Recognizing potential dangers in enclosed spaces is essential to staying safe. Here are some red flags to watch for:

Loitering Individuals: Be cautious of individuals who loiter without a clear purpose, especially in isolated areas like stairwells, restrooms, or hallways. They may be waiting for an opportunity to confront or steal.

Unusual Behavior: Be aware of individuals who exhibit unusual behavior, such as pacing, excessive nervousness, or who appear to be under the influence of drugs or alcohol. These can be signs of potential trouble.

Following or Stalking: If you notice someone consistently appearing in the same areas as you or if someone seems to be following you, take action. Go to a public area, alert security, or call for help.

Restricted or Unauthorized Access: Watch for people trying to access areas they shouldn't be in, such as restricted floors or locked doors. This could indicate an attempt to bypass security.

Manipulating Security Features: Be vigilant of individuals tampering with security cameras, doors, or alarms. These actions suggest preparation for a potential crime.

Inappropriate Questions: Be wary of anyone asking personal questions or inquiring about your movements, such as where you are going or when you will return. This can be a tactic to gather information for later use.

Emergency Exits and Escape Routes

Knowing how to use emergency exits and escape routes is critical in case of fires, natural disasters, or other emergencies. Here's how to prepare:

Familiarize Yourself: As soon as you enter a building, take note of the nearest emergency exits and stairwells. Many buildings have maps near elevators or main entrances; take a moment to review them.

Avoid Elevators During Emergencies: In emergencies such as fires, never use elevators, as they can malfunction or become traps. Use stairwells designated as emergency exits.

Practice Situational Awareness: Always be aware of alternative exits. If the primary route is blocked, know the secondary options, such as other stairwells or windows that can be used for evacuation.

Keep Exits Clear: Never block or obstruct emergency exits with personal belongings, furniture, or other items. Clear exits save time and lives during evacuations.

Emergency Drills: Participate in or review emergency drills if you work or spend significant time in a particular building. Knowing the evacuation procedure can reduce panic and improve response times.

Alert Others if Safe to Do So: If you notice an emergency situation developing, such as a fire or someone acting aggressively, and it is safe to do so, alert others around you. Pull fire alarms or notify security personnel to initiate broader building alerts.

Stay Low in Smoke: If evacuating during a fire, stay low to the ground where the air is clearer and less toxic. Crawl if necessary and cover your mouth and nose with a cloth to filter out smoke.

Check Doors for Heat: Before opening any doors during a fire, check the door's temperature with the back of your hand. A hot door indicates fire on the other side, and you should seek an alternate route.

Emergency Kits: In buildings where you spend a lot of time, consider keeping an emergency kit nearby. Include items like a flashlight, a whistle, bottled water, and a first aid kit. These supplies can be invaluable during extended evacuations or power outages.

By following these guidelines, you can enhance your safety and be better prepared for any situation that may arise within buildings. Being proactive, recognizing red flags, and knowing your escape routes are key components of personal security in enclosed spaces. Always prioritize your safety and be prepared to act swiftly in case of emergencies.

Convenience Stores and Gas Stations

Convenience stores and gas stations are often frequented for their accessibility and quick services. However, these locations can also be high-risk areas due to their 24-hour operations, isolated locations, and frequent cash transactions. To navigate these environments safely, it's crucial to be aware of safety protocols, avoid common mistakes that make you a target, and know how to make quick decisions during unexpected confrontations. This guide provides essential strategies for staying safe at ATMs, convenience stores, and gas stations.

Safety Protocols for High-Risk Areas Like ATMs and Convenience Stores

Convenience stores, gas stations, and ATMs are hotspots for opportunistic crimes such as theft, robbery, and assault. Implementing safety protocols when using these services can significantly reduce your risk.

ATMs:

Choose Safe Locations: Use ATMs located in well-lit, busy areas, preferably indoors or at a bank branch. Avoid standalone ATMs in secluded spots, especially at night, as they are more vulnerable to criminal activity.

Be Aware of Your Surroundings: Before approaching an ATM, scan the area for suspicious individuals or activity. If something feels off, trust your instincts and find another location. Avoid ATMs with people loitering nearby or where visibility is poor.

Protect Your PIN: Shield your PIN by covering the keypad with your hand while entering it. Be cautious of anyone standing too close or attempting to look over your shoulder.

Stay Alert: Keep your focus on your transaction and your surroundings. Avoid distractions such as phone calls or checking messages while using an ATM. Complete your transaction quickly, retrieve your card and cash promptly, and move away from the area.

Have Your Card Ready: Avoid fumbling through your wallet or bag when you reach the ATM. Have your card ready to insert, which reduces your time at the machine and minimizes exposure to potential threats.

Convenience Stores:

Observe Before Entering: Before entering a convenience store, take a moment to observe what's happening inside and outside. Look for signs of distress or any unusual behavior from customers or employees. If something seems off, wait or choose a different store.

Stay Visible: Once inside, stay in well-lit areas and avoid corners or aisles that are out of view. Being in plain sight of store staff and other customers reduces the likelihood of being targeted.

Limit Cash Handling: If possible, use a card instead of cash to minimize exposure when making payments. Avoid counting cash openly or displaying large amounts of money, which can attract unwanted attention.

Avoid Late-Night Visits: Convenience stores can be more dangerous late at night when they are less crowded and more likely to be targeted for crime. If you must visit a convenience store during these hours, try to choose one with visible security measures such as cameras or a security guard.

Gas Stations:

Stay Near Your Vehicle: When pumping gas, stay near your vehicle and keep your keys on you at all times. Lock your doors if you leave your car, even briefly. Avoid going inside the store if you can pay at the pump, as this minimizes your exposure.

Be Aware of "Sliders": Sliders are thieves who slide into your vehicle from the opposite side while you're distracted at the pump. Keep your car doors locked and your valuables out of sight to prevent this type of theft.

Fuel in Safe Locations: Choose gas stations in well-populated, well-lit areas, and avoid those in remote or high-crime neighborhoods. If possible, refuel during the day when there's more activity and better visibility.

Keep a Lookout: Be mindful of individuals who approach you while you're fueling. Common scams include asking for money, directions, or assistance. Politely decline and maintain your distance, especially if the person's behavior seems suspicious.

Avoiding Common Mistakes That Make You a Target

In high-risk areas like ATMs, convenience stores, and gas stations, certain behaviors can inadvertently make you a target for criminals. Avoiding these common mistakes can greatly improve your personal safety.

Being Distracted: Distractions such as phone use, listening to music with headphones, or being overly engrossed in other tasks can make you less aware of your surroundings. This inattentiveness can signal to criminals that you're an easy target. Stay alert and keep your focus on your environment.

Displaying Valuables: Flashing expensive items like smartphones, jewelry, or large amounts of cash can attract attention. Keep valuable items out of sight and secure when in public spaces. If you need to use your phone, do so discreetly and quickly.

Ignoring Your Intuition: Many people ignore their gut feelings when something feels off because they don't want to seem rude or paranoid. However, your intuition is often a reliable indicator of danger. If a situation or person makes you uncomfortable, don't hesitate to leave the area or seek help.

Using ATMs at Night: Using ATMs after dark, especially in secluded locations, increases your risk of becoming a target. Whenever possible, conduct ATM transactions during daylight hours or inside a bank where security measures are stronger.

Leaving Your Vehicle Unsecured: At gas stations or convenience stores, many people leave their vehicles unlocked or even running while they quickly step away. This can make your car an easy target for theft. Always lock your doors, take your keys, and avoid leaving your vehicle unattended.

Engaging with Strangers: While not all strangers have bad intentions, engaging with unknown individuals in high-risk areas can put you at risk. Be cautious of those who approach you with unsolicited offers, requests, or conversations. Politely but firmly decline interactions that seem unnecessary or suspicious.

Quick Decisions for Staying Safe in Unexpected Confrontations

Unexpected confrontations can happen suddenly, leaving little time to think. Knowing how to respond quickly and effectively can help you stay safe.

De-escalate When Possible: If confronted, your first goal should be to de-escalate the situation. Stay calm, avoid making sudden movements, and speak in a non-threatening tone. If someone demands money or valuables, comply without resistance. Your safety is more valuable than your possessions.

Use Your Voice: In some situations, using a firm and assertive voice can deter a potential attacker. Shouting commands like "Back off!" or drawing attention by yelling "Help!" can startle the aggressor and alert others to your distress.

Create Distance: If you feel threatened, create distance between you and the potential aggressor. Move to a more populated area, such as near the cashier in a store or closer to other customers. Distance reduces the immediacy of the threat and increases your chances of getting help.

Keep Your Hands Free: In a confrontation, your ability to use your hands is crucial. Avoid holding items that could be dropped or used against you. If possible, keep one hand on your personal items and the other free to defend yourself or make a quick move.

Know Your Escape Routes: Always be aware of exits and potential escape routes in any high-risk area. Whether in a store, at a gas station, or near an ATM, knowing where you can quickly exit can be a lifesaver in an emergency. If something goes wrong, your priority should be to leave the situation as quickly as possible.

Use Self-Defense Wisely: Self-defense should always be a last resort, used only when you feel your safety is in immediate danger and there is no option to escape. Carrying a personal safety device, such as pepper spray or a whistle, can provide a critical advantage in an emergency. If you decide to carry such items, ensure you know how to use them effectively.

Report Suspicious Activity: If you experience or witness suspicious activity, report it to the authorities immediately. Your actions could prevent a crime and help others stay safe. Provide clear descriptions of suspects, vehicles, and the nature of the incident.

Stay Composed: In any confrontation, staying composed is key. Panic can cloud your judgment and lead to poor decision-making. Take a deep breath, assess the situation quickly, and focus on the safest course of action.

By following these safety protocols, avoiding common mistakes, and knowing how to respond in unexpected confrontations, you can significantly reduce your risk and stay safe in high-risk areas like convenience stores, gas stations, and ATMs. Being prepared and proactive in these environments not only enhances your personal security but also helps you navigate daily tasks with confidence.

Safer on Public Transportation

Public transportation offers a convenient and cost-effective way to travel, but it can also present safety challenges. Whether you're taking the subway, trains, planes, taxis, or ride-shares, being aware of potential risks and knowing how to handle uncomfortable or threatening situations is essential. For solo travelers and those commuting late at night, these challenges can be even greater. This guide provides protocols for staying safe on various forms of public transportation, tips for handling difficult situations, and specific advice for solo travelers and late-night commuters.

Protocols for Subways, Trains, Planes, Taxis, and Ride-Shares

Each mode of public transportation comes with its own set of safety considerations. By following these protocols, you can navigate these environments more securely.

Subways and Trains:

Stay in Well-Lit, Busy Areas: When waiting for subways or trains, stay in well-lit areas where there are other passengers. Platforms can be isolated during off-peak hours, so positioning yourself near station attendants, security personnel, or emergency call boxes can provide an added layer of safety.

Mind Your Belongings: Keep your bags and personal items close to you at all times. Avoid placing bags on the floor or seats where they can be easily snatched. If you need to stand, place your bag between your feet or hold it securely.

Be Aware of Pickpockets: Crowded trains and subways are prime locations for pickpockets. Keep your valuables out of sight, use bags that zip, and avoid keeping wallets in back pockets. Be especially vigilant in crowded spaces where jostling or close contact is common.

Choose the Right Car: When possible, board the first car of the train where the conductor is located. This car is generally safer, especially during off-peak hours. Avoid empty cars, as these can make you more vulnerable to harassment or attack.

Stay Alert: Avoid distractions such as texting or listening to music with both headphones in. Keeping one earbud out or using low volume can help you remain aware of your surroundings. Regularly scan the area for any unusual behavior or potential threats.

Planes:

Secure Your Belongings: Keep important items like passports, wallets, and phones on your person rather than in overhead bins. This reduces the risk of theft during flights or while deplaning.

Be Cautious with Drinks: When traveling on planes, be mindful of your drinks, especially if you're traveling alone. Accept drinks only from flight attendants and never leave your drink unattended.

Know the Exits: Familiarize yourself with the nearest exits and safety procedures outlined by the crew.

Understanding these protocols can be crucial in case of an emergency.

Maintain Personal Boundaries: If someone makes you uncomfortable during the flight, whether through unwanted conversation or physical proximity, politely but firmly assert your boundaries. If necessary, notify a flight attendant, who can assist in resolving the situation or reassigning seats if available.

3. Taxis and Ride-Shares:

Verify Your Ride: Always verify the license plate, driver's name, and car model before getting into a ride-share. Never get into a vehicle that doesn't match the information provided by the app. For added security, ask the driver who they are picking up to confirm that they have your correct details.

Share Your Location: Use the ride-share app's option to share your trip details with a friend or family member. This feature allows someone else to track your journey in real-time, providing an extra layer of security.

Sit in the Back: For taxis and ride-shares, sitting in the back seat provides a safer distance from the driver and allows you to exit from either side of the vehicle. It also gives you more personal space and makes it easier to observe the driver's behavior.

Follow the Route: Pay attention to the route your driver is taking. Use a navigation app on your phone to ensure that the driver is following the correct path. If the driver deviates significantly or makes you uncomfortable, speak up or ask to stop at a safe location.

Emergency Features: Familiarize yourself with emergency features on ride-share apps, such as the panic button, which connects you directly to emergency services. Be prepared to use it if you feel threatened.

Handling Uncomfortable or Threatening Situations During Travel

Unexpected or uncomfortable situations can occur while using public transportation. Knowing how to respond effectively can help you maintain control and safety.

Trust Your Instincts: If a situation feels wrong, trust your instincts. If you sense someone is watching you or making you uncomfortable, move to a different area, such as another train car or a different section of the platform. Your intuition is a powerful tool for staying safe.

Set Boundaries: If someone invades your personal space or makes unwelcome advances, set clear boundaries. A firm "Please leave me alone" or "I'm not interested" can often be enough to deter further interaction. If the behavior continues, don't hesitate to seek help from transportation staff or security personnel.

Use Your Voice: Drawing attention to an uncomfortable or threatening situation can be a powerful deterrent. Loudly asking "What are you doing?" or saying "Stop!" can alert those around you and discourage the aggressor. In more serious situations, don't be afraid to yell for help.

Keep Moving: If you feel threatened, keep moving toward a populated area or seek out transportation personnel. On subways and trains, move to a different car. In airports, head towards security or customer service desks where assistance is readily available.

Document and Report: If you encounter harassment or a threatening situation, try to document details such as the person's appearance, actions, and any identifying features. Reporting these incidents to authorities or transportation staff can help prevent future occurrences.

Have an Exit Strategy: Always be aware of your surroundings and have an exit strategy. This might mean knowing the location of emergency exits, planning your route to the nearest help point, or having an alternative transportation option if you need to leave quickly.

Tips for Solo Travelers and Late-Night Commuting

Traveling alone or late at night can present additional risks, making it crucial to take extra precautions.

Plan Ahead: Plan your route in advance, and know the schedules for subways, buses, or trains to avoid long waits in isolated areas. If possible, avoid the last bus or train of the night, as these are often less crowded and can be more dangerous.

Stay Connected: Keep your phone charged and accessible, and inform a trusted person of your travel plans and expected arrival time. Apps that allow you to share your location can provide an added layer of security.

Choose Well-Lit Stops: Opt for well-lit, busy stops or stations, especially at night. Avoid isolated areas or corners where visibility is poor. If a stop seems unsafe, continue to the next one or seek an alternative route.

Avoid Sleep Deprivation: Fatigue can impair your judgment and reaction time, making you more vulnerable. If you're traveling late, try to stay alert and aware of your surroundings. If you feel tired, engage in activities that keep you awake, such as listening to music or reading.

Carry Personal Safety Devices: Consider carrying a personal safety device such as pepper spray, a whistle, or a personal alarm. These can provide a sense of security and be useful in deterring potential threats.

Use Designated Services: When possible, use designated taxis, ride-shares, or transportation services recommended by your accommodation or local authorities. These services are usually vetted and offer safer options compared to unregulated alternatives.

Avoid Empty Stations: Late at night, empty stations can be hazardous. If you arrive at a station that is deserted, remain near exits or in view of surveillance cameras. If you feel unsafe, consider staying on the train until you reach a busier stop or contact station staff for assistance.

Don't Overshare: While traveling alone, avoid oversharing details of your trip with strangers, including where you are staying or your travel itinerary. This information can be misused if it falls into the wrong hands.

Dress for the Situation: Dress in a way that allows you to move easily and does not attract unnecessary attention. Avoid displaying expensive items like jewelry or high-end electronics, which can make you a target for theft.

Be Confident and Purposeful: Walk with confidence and purpose, even if you're unsure of your surroundings. Criminals are less likely to target individuals who appear assertive and aware of their environment.

By following these protocols, handling difficult situations proactively, and taking extra precautions when traveling solo or late at night, you can significantly enhance your safety on public transportation. Staying alert, prepared, and aware of your surroundings is key to navigating these environments securely and confidently.

Safer at Restaurants and Bars

Restaurants and bars are popular social settings where people gather to eat, drink, and enjoy the company of others. While these environments can be fun and relaxing, they also present unique safety challenges, especially where alcohol is involved. Being mindful of your surroundings, recognizing predatory behavior, and managing your personal safety in crowded and noisy environments are essential skills. This guide provides practical tips for navigating these social settings, identifying and avoiding potential dangers, and maintaining your safety in busy establishments.

Navigating Social Settings Where Alcohol Is Served

Social settings where alcohol is served can lower inhibitions and impair judgment, making it easier for accidents or unwanted incidents to occur. Understanding how to navigate these environments safely is crucial for protecting yourself and enjoying your time out.

Drink Responsibly:

Know Your Limits: Drinking responsibly is the first step in ensuring your safety. Know your alcohol tolerance and pace yourself to avoid becoming overly intoxicated. Drinking water between alcoholic beverages can help you stay hydrated and maintain better control.

Watch Your Drink: Never leave your drink unattended, as it could be tampered with. Always keep your drink in sight and avoid accepting drinks from strangers unless you see them being made by a bartender. Consider using drink covers or test strips that detect common date-rape drugs for added safety.

Plan Your Transportation: Arrange a safe way to get home before you start drinking. Use designated drivers, ride-share services, or public transportation. Avoid walking home alone, especially if you're in an unfamiliar area or if you've been drinking.

Stick with Friends:

Stay Together: There's safety in numbers. Stick with friends or trusted companions, especially when moving between locations. Make a plan to look out for each other, and agree on a designated meeting point in case someone gets separated.

Communicate: Keep in touch with your group throughout the night. Use group messaging apps to stay connected, and check in periodically. If you decide to leave early or go somewhere else, inform your friends of your plans.

Be Aware of Your Surroundings:

Scout the Location: When you arrive at a bar or restaurant, take a moment to familiarize yourself with the layout, including exits, restrooms, and areas with good visibility. Knowing the environment can help you act quickly in case of an emergency.

Avoid Overcrowded Areas: Overcrowded spaces can increase the risk of accidents, altercations, or theft. If possible, choose seating in less congested areas where you have a clear view of the surroundings and easy access to exits.

Limit Sharing Personal Information: Be mindful of how much personal information you share with strangers. Avoid discussing details like where you live, your plans for the night, or your relationship status, as this information can be misused.

Recognizing and Avoiding Predatory Behavior

Predatory behavior can take many forms in social settings, from unwanted advances to more subtle attempts at manipulation. Recognizing these behaviors and knowing how to respond can help protect you from harm.

Trust Your Instincts:

Listen to Your Gut: If someone makes you uncomfortable, trust your instincts. Predatory behavior often involves subtle boundary violations, such as invading your personal space, making inappropriate comments, or refusing to take no for an answer. If something feels off, don't hesitate to distance yourself or seek help.

Be Assertive: Clearly communicate your boundaries and be firm if someone is making you uncomfortable. Responses like "I'm not interested" or "Please leave me alone" can be effective. If the person persists, don't be afraid to escalate the situation by alerting friends, staff, or security.

Watch for Red Flags:

Isolating Behavior: Predators may try to isolate you from your friends or the group, often under the guise of wanting to talk privately or offering to buy you a drink elsewhere. Stay with your group, and if someone insists on separating you, recognize this as a red flag.

Excessive Generosity: While it's common for people to buy drinks in social settings, excessive generosity or insistence on paying for everything can be a tactic to make you feel indebted or obligated. Accept offers cautiously, and never feel compelled to reciprocate in ways that make you uncomfortable.

Intense or Rapid Engagement: Be wary of individuals who push for quick intimacy or become overly personal too soon. This could include asking probing questions, sharing overly personal stories to gain sympathy, or pressuring you to drink or leave with them.

Use the Buddy System:

Look Out for Each Other: Agree with friends to watch each other's backs. If someone notices predatory behavior, step in by redirecting the conversation or suggesting a change of location. Having a pre-arranged signal or code word can help communicate discomfort discreetly.

Involve Staff: If you're feeling threatened or harassed, don't hesitate to involve restaurant or bar staff. Most establishments take patron safety seriously and will assist in managing the situation, whether it involves asking someone to leave or calling security.

Managing Personal Safety in Crowded and Noisy Environments

Crowded and noisy environments like busy bars or restaurants can make it difficult to stay aware of your surroundings, which can increase your vulnerability. Here are some tips to help you manage your safety in these settings:

Keep Your Personal Items Secure:

Use Crossbody Bags or Zipped Pockets: Keep your belongings close and secure. Crossbody bags are harder to snatch than purses or shoulder bags, and zipped pockets reduce the risk of pickpocketing. Keep valuables like phones and wallets tucked away and out of sight.

Be Aware of Your Space: In crowded environments, it's easy for someone to invade your space without you noticing. Be mindful of those around you, and if someone is standing too close, reposition yourself or move to a less crowded area.

Stay in Control of Your Drink:

Know Your Drink: Order your own drinks and watch them being made. If you lose track of your drink, don't take the risk—order a new one. Be especially cautious with shared drinks like pitchers or punch bowls, as these can be more easily tampered with.

Avoid Accepting Drinks from Strangers: Accepting drinks from strangers can be risky, as you cannot be sure of their intentions. If you do accept, ensure the drink is handed to you directly from the bartender.

Use Technology Wisely:

Set Up Safety Apps: Use safety apps that allow you to quickly notify friends or emergency services if you're in trouble. Many apps offer features like one-touch alerts, live location sharing, or even fake call features to help you exit uncomfortable situations.

Share Your Location: Before heading out, share your real-time location with a trusted friend or family member. This allows them to check in on you and ensures someone knows where you are.

Control Your Environment:

Choose Strategic Seating: When possible, choose seats that provide a clear view of the entrance and exits. This position allows you to observe who comes and goes, and it provides a quicker path out if needed.

Stay Near Exits: In noisy or crowded settings, stay near exits so you can leave quickly if necessary. Avoid seating in secluded corners or areas with poor visibility, as these can make it harder for you to spot potential threats or get help.

Prepare for Emergencies:

Identify Emergency Exits: Upon entering a venue, take note of emergency exits. Knowing where they are can save precious time in case of a fire, altercation, or other emergencies.

Have a Backup Plan: Always have a backup plan in case your original transportation arrangements fall through. Keep a charged phone with contact numbers for taxi services or ride-share apps, and know alternative ways to get home.

Manage Noise and Sensory Overload:

Stay Grounded: In loud and chaotic environments, it's easy to become disoriented or overwhelmed. If you start to feel anxious or uncomfortable, step outside for a moment to regain your composure. Fresh air and a quieter space can help you reset and maintain control.

Limit Alcohol Intake: Excessive noise combined with alcohol can impair your judgment and response time. By moderating your alcohol intake, you'll remain more aware of your surroundings and better equipped to handle any situation that arises.

Navigating restaurants and bars safely requires awareness, assertiveness, and preparation. By understanding how to recognize predatory behavior, manage your personal space, and maintain control in social settings, you can enjoy your time out while keeping yourself protected. Whether you're alone or with friends, these strategies will help you make the most of your night without compromising your safety.

Safer While Traveling

Traveling, whether for business or pleasure, offers the excitement of new experiences and places. However, it also comes with unique safety challenges, especially in unfamiliar environments where you might be more vulnerable to scams, theft, or other dangers. Whether you're on a business trip or vacation, following safety protocols, staying vigilant, and being prepared can help ensure a smooth and secure journey. This guide provides essential safety protocols for travel, tips for staying secure in unfamiliar locations, and strategies for handling travel-related scams and thefts.

Safety Protocols for Business Trips and Vacations

Regardless of the purpose of your travel, following basic safety protocols can help you minimize risks and protect your personal security. Here are some strategies to consider before and during your trip:

Research Your Destination:

Understand the Local Environment: Before you travel, research your destination thoroughly. Learn about the local culture, customs, and any potential safety concerns. Check travel advisories, and be aware of high-risk areas to avoid, such as neighborhoods with high crime rates or political unrest.

Know Emergency Contacts: Familiarize yourself with local emergency numbers, the nearest embassy or consulate, and healthcare facilities. Having these contacts readily available can be crucial in case of an emergency.

Secure Your Accommodations:

Choose Safe Accommodations: Select hotels or rentals in safe, well-populated areas. Read reviews to gauge the experiences of other travelers, and prioritize places that have good security measures in place, such as 24-hour front desk service, secure entry points, and surveillance cameras.

Inspect Your Room: Upon arrival, inspect your room's locks, windows, and other entry points to ensure they are secure. If something feels unsafe, request a room change or consider moving to a different hotel.

Use Hotel Safes Wisely: Use the hotel safe for valuables, but avoid placing items in the safe that you can't afford to lose. It's also advisable to use a personal travel safe for important documents and electronics.

Keep a Low Profile:

Blend In: Avoid standing out as a tourist, which can make you a target for scams and theft. Dress modestly, refrain from displaying expensive items like jewelry or cameras, and avoid discussing your travel plans loudly in public spaces.

Limit Social Media Sharing: While it's tempting to share your travel experiences in real-time, consider waiting until after your trip to post photos and updates. Broadcasting your location publicly can make you more vulnerable to theft, especially if your home is unoccupied.

Maintain Travel Safety Practices:

Secure Your Belongings: Keep your personal items, such as your passport, wallet, and phone, secure at all times. Use anti-theft bags with lockable zippers and keep your belongings close to your body. Avoid placing valuables in easily accessible outer pockets.

Stay Vigilant in Transit: Whether you're flying, taking a train, or using other forms of transit, keep an eye on your belongings and be cautious of those around you. Avoid falling asleep in unsecured areas or leaving your bags unattended.

Stay Connected:

Share Your Itinerary: Share your travel itinerary, accommodation details, and contact information with a trusted friend or family member. Regularly check in with them, especially if you're traveling solo or in a high-risk area.

Keep Devices Charged: Always have a fully charged phone with you, and consider carrying a portable charger. A functioning phone can be your lifeline in emergencies, providing access to navigation, communication, and safety apps.

Tips for Staying Secure in Unfamiliar Locations

Unfamiliar locations can be disorienting and sometimes unsafe. By adopting these strategies, you can enhance your security while exploring new places:

Be Aware of Your Surroundings:

Stay Alert: Pay attention to your environment at all times. Look for exits, observe the behavior of those around you, and be mindful of potential hazards. If something feels off, trust your instincts and leave the area.

Avoid Distractions: Limit distractions, such as excessive phone use or wearing headphones, especially when navigating crowded or unfamiliar areas. Staying present and aware can help you spot potential dangers early.

Use Reliable Transportation:

Choose Safe Transport Options: Use reputable transportation services, such as licensed taxis, official ride-shares, or hotel-provided shuttles. Avoid unmarked taxis or accepting rides from strangers, as these can pose significant risks.

Know Your Route: Before setting off, familiarize yourself with the route to your destination. Use navigation apps to monitor your journey and ensure your driver is taking the correct path. If something seems amiss, speak up or request to stop in a safe location.

Protect Your Personal Information:

Be Cautious with Public Wi-Fi: Public Wi-Fi networks can be vulnerable to hackers. Avoid accessing sensitive information, such as bank accounts or personal emails, on unsecured networks. Use a virtual private network (VPN) to protect your data when using public Wi-Fi.

Guard Against Eavesdropping: Be mindful of your conversations in public spaces. Avoid discussing sensitive details, such as your travel plans or personal information, where others can overhear.

Manage Your Cash and Cards:

Use Multiple Payment Methods: Carry a mix of payment methods, including cash, credit cards, and a backup card. Keep them in different locations, such as your wallet, a hidden money belt, and your hotel safe, to minimize loss if one is stolen.

Limit Cash Carrying: Avoid carrying large amounts of cash. Withdraw small amounts as needed, and use cards for larger transactions. This reduces the risk of losing significant sums of money if you're targeted by thieves.

Stay in Well-Lit, Busy Areas:

Avoid Isolation: Stick to busy, well-lit areas, especially at night. Avoid shortcuts through alleys, deserted streets, or unfamiliar neighborhoods where you could be more vulnerable to crime.

Know the Local Culture: Understanding local customs and social norms can help you blend in and avoid inadvertently offending locals or attracting unwanted attention. Respect local dress codes, especially in conservative areas, and be polite in your interactions.

Handling Travel-Related Scams and Thefts

Scams and thefts are common risks for travelers, particularly in tourist-heavy areas. Being prepared and knowing how to handle these situations can help you avoid becoming a victim.

Recognize Common Scams:

Distraction Scams: Be wary of individuals who create distractions, such as spilling something on you or causing a commotion. These tactics are often used by pickpockets or accomplices working together to steal from unsuspecting travelers.

Overcharging Scams: Taxi drivers, street vendors, and other service providers may attempt to overcharge tourists. To avoid this, agree on prices beforehand, use meters in taxis, and familiarize yourself with local currency to quickly identify correct amounts.

Fake Officials: Be cautious of individuals posing as police officers or other officials who request to see your documents or demand fines. Always ask for identification and, if in doubt, offer to accompany them to the nearest police station to verify their legitimacy.

Protect Your Valuables:

Use Anti-Theft Gear: Invest in anti-theft gear, such as slash-resistant bags, money belts, and locks for your luggage. These can deter pickpockets and opportunistic thieves from accessing your belongings.

Keep Copies of Important Documents: Photocopy your passport, visas, and other critical documents, and store them separately from the originals. Digital copies can also be kept in a secure cloud service for easy access if needed.

Responding to Theft:

Report Immediately: If you are a victim of theft, report it to local authorities and your accommodation as soon as possible. Obtain a police report, as it may be required for insurance claims or when replacing stolen items, such as passports.

Cancel Cards and Secure Accounts: If your wallet or cards are stolen, contact your bank immediately to cancel the cards and secure your accounts. Having a list of emergency contact numbers for your bank can expedite this process.

Be Skeptical of "Helpers":

Unsolicited Assistance: Be cautious of strangers offering unsolicited help, such as carrying your bags, offering directions, or providing unsolicited tours. While some offers may be genuine, they can also be attempts to distract or scam you.

Check Your Change: When making purchases, always check your change and receipts carefully. Some vendors may attempt to shortchange tourists or charge higher prices than agreed.

Protect Your Accommodation:

Secure Your Room: Use the door's security features, such as deadbolts and chains, and avoid opening the door to strangers. If someone claims to be from hotel staff, verify with the front desk before allowing entry.

Don't Advertise Your Absence: Avoid placing the "clean my room" sign on your hotel door, as it indicates your absence. Instead, call housekeeping when you're ready for the room to be cleaned.

Plan for the Unexpected:

Travel Insurance: Consider purchasing travel insurance that covers theft, medical emergencies, and trip cancellations. This can provide peace of mind and financial protection in case of unforeseen incidents.

Keep Emergency Funds: Store a small amount of emergency cash in a secure location, separate from your wallet. This can be a lifesaver if your primary funds are lost or stolen.

By following these safety protocols, staying vigilant in unfamiliar locations, and being prepared to handle scams and thefts, you can enhance your safety and enjoy a more secure travel experience. Whether on a business trip or vacation, being proactive about your security allows you to focus on the pleasures of exploring new places while minimizing risks.

Safer When Lodging

When traveling, your choice of lodging can significantly impact your overall safety. Whether you're staying in a hotel, motel, hostel, or Airbnb, it's important to take steps to ensure your personal security and protect your belongings. By choosing accommodations with the right security features, selecting safer rooms, and following practical safety tips, you can minimize risks and enjoy a more secure stay. This guide provides essential advice for staying safe when lodging away from home.

Hotel, Motel, Hostel, and Airbnb Safety Tips

Each type of accommodation comes with its own unique set of safety considerations. By being mindful of these differences and following these general safety tips, you can enhance your security no matter where you stay.

Hotels:

Choose Reputable Brands: Whenever possible, choose well-known hotels with good reputations for safety and security. Major hotel chains often have standardized safety protocols, including 24-hour front desk service, security personnel, and surveillance systems.

Avoid Ground Floor Rooms: Rooms on the ground floor are more accessible to intruders. Request a room between the third and sixth floors—high enough to deter easy access from outside, but low enough for fire escape ladders to reach.

Check Room Security: Ensure that your room has a sturdy deadbolt, a peephole, and a security chain or latch on the door. If any of these features are missing or damaged, request a different room. Always use these security features when inside your room.

Use the Hotel Safe: For valuables like passports, electronics, or extra cash, use the in-room safe if it's available. If you have doubts about the safety of the room safe, ask the front desk about using a secure safe deposit box.

Be Aware of Door Etiquette: Never open your door to strangers, even if they claim to be hotel staff. Verify their identity by calling the front desk. Use the peephole to see who is at the door before opening it, and keep the security latch engaged until you're sure it's safe.

Motels:

Choose Well-Lit Motels: When selecting a motel, opt for one with good lighting in the parking lot and common areas. Well-lit environments deter criminal activity and make it easier for you to spot any suspicious behavior.

Park Close to Your Room: Try to park your vehicle near your room, preferably within your line of sight. This not only provides convenience but also allows you to keep an eye on your car, reducing the risk of theft or vandalism.

Check Locks and Windows: Motels often have external doors, so it's crucial to ensure that both the door and windows are secure. Check that locks work properly and that windows are either locked or have a secondary locking mechanism.

Avoid Posting Your Room Number: Be discreet with your room number. Avoid loudly stating it in public areas and never display it on your key card sleeve. If the motel uses key cards, keep them safe and immediately report lost or stolen cards to the front desk.

Hostels:

Use Lockers for Valuables: Hostels usually provide lockers for guests. Always use these lockers for valuables and secure them with your own lock rather than relying on hostel-provided locks, which may be less secure.

Be Selective About Dorm Rooms: If possible, choose dorm rooms with fewer beds. Smaller rooms typically offer more privacy and security. If traveling alone, consider opting for female-only or mixed-gender dorms based on your comfort level.

Know Your Roommates: While it's not always feasible to know your roommates well in a hostel, being friendly and aware of who is staying in your room can help you spot anything unusual. Report any suspicious behavior to hostel staff.

Keep Personal Items Close: Keep your personal belongings close to your bed while you sleep. Use a travel pouch or money belt to keep important items like your phone, wallet, and passport secure.

Airbnb and Vacation Rentals:

Choose Verified Listings: Book through reputable platforms like Airbnb, and choose listings with verified hosts, positive reviews, and high ratings. Read past guest reviews carefully to gauge the host's reliability and the safety of the location.

Check Safety Features: Look for listings that mention safety features like smoke detectors, carbon monoxide detectors, first aid kits, and secure locks. If this information isn't available in the listing, ask the host directly before booking.

Meet the Host in Public: If the host will meet you to provide keys, arrange to meet in a public place rather than at the property. This provides an added layer of security and ensures that you're comfortable before entering the accommodation.

Secure the Property: Upon arrival, check the property's doors and windows to ensure they lock properly. If you're staying in an apartment or house, be mindful of who can access shared spaces, and use any available security systems.

Checking for Security Features and Choosing Safer Rooms

Choosing a room with appropriate security features is a key aspect of staying safe while lodging. Here are some tips for evaluating security features and selecting safer rooms:

Room Location:

Avoid Rooms at the End of Hallways: Rooms at the end of hallways or near emergency exits can be more vulnerable to intruders. Mid-hallway rooms are generally safer as they have more visibility and foot traffic.

Consider Elevator Proximity: While rooms close to elevators can be noisy, they also provide quick access to exits and are often more secure due to increased foot traffic and surveillance.

Evaluate Security Features:

Check Surveillance and Lighting: Look for visible surveillance cameras in hallways, parking lots, and public areas. Good lighting in these areas is also crucial for safety. If the hotel or rental lacks these features, it may be a sign of inadequate security.

Door and Window Locks: Make sure doors have robust locks, including deadbolts and security chains. Windows should have locks, and any sliding doors should have secondary security features like bars or rods.

Fire Safety: Check for smoke alarms, fire extinguishers, and clear fire escape plans. Knowing where fire exits are located can be vital in an emergency.

Secure Your Room:

Use Door Stops or Portable Locks: Consider bringing a portable door lock or a rubber doorstop to provide additional security from inside your room. These are inexpensive and easy to carry in your luggage.

Block Peepholes: If your room has a peephole, make sure it's covered when not in use to prevent anyone from looking in. Some hotels provide peephole covers, but if not, a piece of tape can work as a temporary measure.

Protecting Your Belongings and Personal Safety When Away from Home

Protecting your belongings and personal safety while lodging is crucial to a worry-free trip. Here are some additional measures to consider:

Keep Valuables Secure:

Carry Minimal Valuables: Only bring what you need. Leave expensive jewelry, unnecessary electronics, and other valuables at home. When traveling, keep critical items like passports, cash, and credit cards close to you in a money belt or secure pouch.

Use Discreet Luggage: Avoid flashy or branded luggage that might signal wealth. Opt for nondescript bags that don't attract attention. Keep your luggage locked, even when it's in your room.

Be Smart with Room Access:

Limit Room Access: If you don't need daily housekeeping, use the "Do Not Disturb" sign to deter staff from entering your room. This minimizes the number of people who access your room and can help prevent theft.

Be Cautious with Room Service: When ordering room service or maintenance, verify that the person at your door is indeed a hotel employee. If in doubt, call the front desk to confirm.

Personal Safety Habits:

Avoid Sharing Too Much: Avoid sharing too much information about your travel plans, room number, or personal details with strangers. Keep your interactions professional and be cautious with anyone who asks probing questions.

Stay Sober: If you plan to drink, do so responsibly. Being overly intoxicated can impair your judgment and make you more vulnerable to theft, assault, or other dangers.

Have Emergency Numbers Ready: Keep a list of emergency contacts, including local emergency numbers, hotel front desk, and nearby friends or family members. Program these numbers into your phone and keep a written copy as a backup.

Be Prepared for Emergencies:

Have a Go-Bag: Prepare a small bag with essentials like a flashlight, a portable charger, water, and basic first aid supplies. Keep this bag accessible in case you need to leave your room quickly due to an emergency.

Know the Exits: Always take note of the nearest emergency exits when you first arrive at your lodging. Familiarize yourself with the route to these exits and ensure that they are unobstructed and clearly marked.

By following these safety tips, checking for key security features, and taking proactive measures to protect your belongings, you can significantly enhance your safety when staying in hotels, motels, hostels, or Airbnbs. Being vigilant and prepared helps ensure that your lodging experience is secure and stress-free, allowing you to focus on enjoying your travels.

Safer in Crowds and at Events

Attending festivals, concerts, sporting events, and other large gatherings can be thrilling experiences. However, these events also come with unique safety challenges due to the high density of people, potential for chaos, and increased risk of incidents such as accidents, altercations, or emergencies. To ensure a safe and enjoyable experience, it's important to follow specific protocols for crowded environments, recognize and avoid dangerous situations, and be prepared with strategies to quickly escape if trouble arises. This guide provides essential tips for staying safe in crowds and at events.

Protocols for Festivals, Concerts, and Sporting Events

Each type of event comes with its own set of dynamics and potential risks, but there are general safety protocols that apply to all large gatherings. By following these guidelines, you can minimize your risks and maximize your enjoyment.

Plan Ahead:

Know the Venue Layout: Before attending an event, familiarize yourself with the layout of the venue. Review maps to identify key locations such as entrances, exits, restrooms, medical stations, and information booths. Knowing these areas will help you navigate the venue more confidently and respond more quickly in an emergency.

Arrive Early: Arriving early can help you avoid the initial rush of crowds and allow you to choose a safer, more comfortable spot. Early arrival also provides the opportunity to scope out your surroundings and plan your exit routes.

Keep Essentials Handy: Carry essential items such as identification, a fully charged phone, a small amount of cash, and emergency contact information. Consider bringing a portable phone charger, as crowded events can quickly drain battery life if you're using your phone frequently for photos, navigation, or communication.

Dress Appropriately:

Wear Comfortable Clothing: Choose comfortable clothing and shoes that are suitable for standing and walking for extended periods. Avoid wearing loose items that could get caught or pulled in a crowd. For outdoor events, consider weather-appropriate attire, such as sun protection or rain gear.

Minimize Valuables: Limit the number of valuables you bring. Leave expensive jewelry and unnecessary electronics at home, and carry only what you need. Use a secure, anti-theft bag with zippers and keep it close to your body to reduce the risk of pickpocketing.

Stay Hydrated and Nourished:

Drink Water: Crowds and high-energy activities can quickly lead to dehydration, especially in hot weather. Drink water regularly and avoid excessive alcohol consumption, which can impair judgment and increase vulnerability.

Eat Light: Eat light, balanced meals before attending events to maintain your energy levels. Heavy meals can lead to fatigue, making it harder to stay alert in a busy, crowded environment.

Stay Connected:

Establish Meeting Points: If attending with a group, designate a specific meeting point in case you get separated. This spot should be easy to find and away from the densest parts of the crowd. Periodically check in with your group to ensure everyone's safety.

Share Your Location: Use phone apps that allow you to share your real-time location with friends or family. This feature is particularly useful if you are attending the event alone or if there is a risk of getting separated in a large crowd.

Avoiding Dangerous Situations in Large Gatherings

Large gatherings can sometimes become unpredictable, making it essential to recognize and avoid dangerous situations. Here are strategies to help you stay out of harm's way:

Stay Aware of Your Surroundings:

Scan the Crowd: Regularly scan your surroundings for any signs of unusual behavior or potential threats. Look out for people acting erratically, aggressive altercations, or any disturbances that could escalate into a larger issue.

Avoid High-Risk Areas: Steer clear of high-risk areas such as densely packed sections near the stage, exits, or concession stands, where crowd surges are more likely. If you feel the crowd getting too tight, move to a less congested area.

Be Mindful of Personal Space:

Maintain a Safe Distance: Keep a buffer of personal space around you when possible. Avoid getting too close to barriers, walls, or other structures that could trap you if the crowd shifts suddenly. If someone is encroaching on your space, gently reposition yourself to maintain a comfortable distance.

Don't Get Caught in the Middle: Position yourself near the edge of the crowd, where it's easier to exit if needed. Avoid being in the middle of densely packed areas, which can become dangerous in the event of a surge or panic.

Recognize Early Signs of Trouble:

Monitor Crowd Dynamics: Pay attention to the overall mood and movement of the crowd. Signs of pushing, shouting, or sudden movement can indicate that tensions are rising. If you notice a shift in the crowd's behavior, prepare to move to a safer location.

Identify Potential Hazards: Be aware of potential hazards such as uneven ground, loose cables, or temporary structures that could pose tripping risks.

Avoid standing near anything that could collapse or block your path in an emergency.

Keep Calm and Avoid Conflicts:

Stay Calm: Crowds can be stressful, but it's important to stay calm and composed. Avoid engaging in arguments or confrontations with others, as these can quickly escalate in a crowded environment. If someone is behaving aggressively, move away and notify event security if necessary.

Use Your Voice: If you feel uncomfortable or need to draw attention to a situation, use your voice. Shouting "Help!" or "Stop!" can alert those around you and deter potential threats. In some cases, loud noise alone can diffuse a situation by drawing attention to it.

Strategies for Escaping Quickly If Trouble Arises

Knowing how to exit quickly and safely from a crowded event can be life-saving if trouble arises. Here are key strategies for making a swift escape:

Have an Exit Plan:

Identify Multiple Exits: Upon arrival, identify the primary exits and any secondary exits that could serve as alternative escape routes. Crowds often head toward the main exit in an emergency, so knowing alternative routes can help you avoid bottlenecks.

Stay Light and Mobile: Keep your belongings minimal and easy to carry. A hands-free bag, such as a crossbody or backpack, allows you to move more quickly and keeps your hands free for balance and navigation.

Move with the Flow of the Crowd:

Follow the Crowd Movement: In emergencies, it's usually safer to move with the flow of the crowd rather than against it. Moving against the crowd can lead to falls or injuries. Instead, look for ways to angle yourself towards the exit while keeping pace with the crowd.

Stay on Your Feet: If you fall, get up quickly. Use your hands and knees if needed, and avoid grabbing onto others, which could pull them down as well. If you can't stand up immediately, curl into a ball and cover your head and neck until you can safely get up.

Avoid Obstructions:

Stay Clear of Barriers: Avoid standing near barriers, fences, or walls where you could become trapped in a surge. If you're near a barrier and the crowd starts to push, move away as quickly as possible.

Be Aware of Structural Hazards: In the case of a fire, structural collapse, or other hazards, move away from the affected area without hesitation. Even seemingly minor damage to temporary stages, scaffolding, or other structures can pose serious risks in a crowded environment.

Use Designated Emergency Exits:

Don't Rely on the Main Exit: In an emergency, the main exit is often the most congested. Instead, use designated emergency exits or alternative paths that you identified earlier. Emergency exits are usually less crowded and designed to handle quick evacuations.

Follow Instructions: Listen for instructions from event staff, security, or emergency personnel. They are trained to manage evacuations and will guide attendees to safety. Stay calm, follow their directions, and avoid pushing or shoving, which can increase the risk of injury.

Communicate with Your Group:

Stay Together: If you're with a group, try to stay together during an emergency. Hold hands or link arms to avoid getting separated. If you do get separated, proceed to your pre-designated meeting point outside the venue.

Use Signals: Agree on simple signals or calls with your group that can be used in noisy environments. A whistle, distinct shout, or even a bright piece of clothing can help you find each other quickly in a crowd.

Prepare for Delays:

Be Patient but Persistent: Exiting a crowded venue can take time, especially if everyone is trying to leave simultaneously. Stay patient, keep moving, and avoid panic. Your goal is to move steadily towards safety without contributing to the chaos.

Stay Informed: Keep an eye on official event communications through loudspeakers, screens, or staff announcements. Staying informed can help you make better decisions during an evacuation.

By following these protocols, staying alert to potential dangers, and having an exit strategy, you can significantly enhance your safety at crowded events. Whether attending a concert, festival, or sporting event, being prepared and aware allows you to enjoy the experience while minimizing risks and ensuring a safer outing.

Part 3: Protecting Against Theft and Scams

Safer from Thieves

Whether you're at home, traveling, or just going about your daily routine, the threat of theft is a common concern. Pick-pocketing, purse-snatching, and phone theft are frequent crimes that can happen quickly and leave you feeling vulnerable. Learning how to protect your valuables, recognizing common theft tactics, and adopting proactive measures can significantly reduce your risk of becoming a victim. This guide provides essential tips for preventing theft, safely carrying valuables, and recognizing and avoiding common theft tactics.

Preventing Pick-Pocketing, Purse-Snatching, and Phone Theft

Thieves often target easy opportunities, such as distracted individuals or those carrying valuables in accessible places. By staying vigilant and adopting preventive measures, you can make yourself a less attractive target.

Stay Vigilant and Aware:

Be Mindful of Your Surroundings: One of the best ways to avoid theft is to remain aware of your surroundings, especially in crowded areas like public transportation, markets, and tourist attractions. Thieves often work in teams and rely on distractions to pick-pocket or snatch valuables without being noticed. Regularly scan your environment and be alert to any unusual or suspicious behavior.

Avoid Distractions: Limit distractions like phone use, listening to music with headphones, or engaging in intense conversations while in public. Thieves prey on people who are not paying attention, so keeping your focus on your surroundings can help deter them.

Secure Your Belongings:

Use Anti-Theft Bags: Invest in bags specifically designed to prevent theft, such as those with lockable zippers, slash-resistant straps, and hidden compartments. Crossbody bags that can be worn in front of your body are generally safer than shoulder bags or backpacks, which are easier to access without your notice.

Keep Bags Closed and Close: Always keep your bags zipped or closed, and hold them close to your body. In crowded spaces, position bags in front of you where you can see them, rather than behind or at your side.

Avoid Back Pockets: Never keep valuables like wallets, phones, or keys in your back pockets. These are the easiest spots for pick-pockets to access. Instead, use front pockets or inner jacket pockets that are harder for thieves to reach.

Protect Your Phone:

Keep Your Phone Out of Sight: When not in use, keep your phone in a secure pocket or bag rather than carrying it in your hand or placing it on a table. Thieves often snatch phones right out of people's hands, especially when they are distracted or preoccupied.

Use Security Features: Enable security features on your phone, such as passcodes, biometric locks, and tracking apps like "Find My Phone." These features make it more difficult for thieves to access your personal information if your phone is stolen.

Avoid Using Your Phone in Crowds: If you need to use your phone in a crowded or unfamiliar area, be discreet. Thieves look for distracted phone users as easy targets, so keeping phone use minimal in public can reduce your risk.

Dress Appropriately:

Minimize Flashy Displays: Avoid wearing expensive jewelry, designer items, or anything that draws unnecessary attention. Flashy displays of wealth can make you a more attractive target for thieves. Instead, opt for understated attire and accessories.

Distribute Your Valuables: Spread your valuables across different pockets or bags to minimize loss if you're targeted. For example, keep some cash in your wallet, some in a hidden money belt, and additional cards in a separate location. This strategy ensures that even if one item is stolen, you don't lose everything.

How to Carry Valuables Safely

Carrying valuables safely requires careful planning and the right tools. By choosing the best methods for storing and carrying your items, you can keep them secure and reduce your risk of theft.

Use Money Belts and Pouches:

Wear Hidden Money Belts: Money belts worn under clothing are an effective way to carry cash, cards, and important documents discreetly. They make it difficult for thieves to access your valuables without your knowledge. Choose a belt that is comfortable, breathable, and lies flat against your body.

Use Neck Pouches and Leg Wallets: In addition to money belts, consider neck pouches or leg wallets that can be worn under your clothing. These options provide alternative ways to carry valuables securely and out of sight.

Choose the Right Bag:

Opt for Crossbody Bags: Crossbody bags are generally safer than handbags or backpacks because they are harder to snatch. Wear the bag across your body with the strap positioned on the opposite shoulder, and keep it in front of you.

Select Bags with Anti-Theft Features: Look for bags with lockable zippers, RFID-blocking technology, and cut-resistant materials. These features make it much more difficult for thieves to access your belongings.

Use Locking Mechanisms: If your bag doesn't have built-in locking zippers, consider using small combination locks or carabiners to secure the zippers together. This simple addition can deter pickpockets from attempting to open your bag.

Secure Your Pockets:

Use Front Pockets: When possible, keep valuables in front pockets rather than back pockets, which are much easier for thieves to access. Pockets with zippers or buttons provide added security.

Wear Clothes with Hidden Pockets: Consider clothing with hidden pockets designed for travel. These pockets are less accessible to thieves and provide a discreet way to carry items like cash, credit cards, and small electronics.

Handle Cash Wisely:

Carry Small Amounts of Cash: Only carry as much cash as you need for the day. If you need to access more cash, use ATMs located inside banks or other secure locations rather than street-side machines.

Divide Your Money: Split your money into different places—some in your wallet, some in a money belt, and some in a safe place at your accommodation. This way, if one stash is compromised, you still have access to funds.

Recognizing and Avoiding Common Theft Tactics

Thieves often use specific tactics to distract, confuse, or catch their victims off guard. By recognizing these methods, you can be better prepared to avoid them.

Distraction Techniques:

The Bump and Grab: Thieves may bump into you or create a commotion to divert your attention while an accomplice steals your valuables. Be cautious of sudden contact or any attempt to draw your focus away from your belongings.

The Fake Spill: Another common tactic involves someone spilling a drink or food on you and then "helping" you clean up, all while lifting your wallet or phone. If this happens, hold onto your belongings and step back immediately.

Crowded Spaces:

Crowd Surges and Bottlenecks: Thieves take advantage of crowded spaces, especially at entrances, exits, and during crowd surges. Keep your bags secured and in front of you during these times, and avoid getting too close to others.

Packed Public Transportation: Public transportation is a hotspot for theft, especially during peak hours when trains and buses are packed. Keep your bag in front of you, hold onto your phone tightly, and avoid standing near the doors where thieves can make a quick escape.

Confidence Scams:

Friendly Strangers: Be wary of overly friendly strangers who offer unsolicited help, directions, or gifts. While many people are genuinely kind, some may be using this as a tactic to distract or scam you.

Street Performers and Crowds: While street performers can be entertaining, they can also attract large crowds where pickpockets thrive. If you stop to watch a performance, be extra vigilant about your belongings, and keep an eye on those around you.

The Grab and Run:

Quick Snatches: Thieves may snatch phones, bags, or other valuables from your hands and run. This is common in outdoor cafes, near train doors, or in busy tourist areas. Keep a firm grip on your items and be mindful of your surroundings, especially when sitting near the street.

Motorcycle or Bicycle Theft: In some cities, thieves on motorcycles or bicycles will ride close to pedestrians and snatch bags or phones. When walking near the street, keep your valuables on the side furthest from traffic to reduce the risk of drive-by thefts.

ATM Scams:

Card Skimming: Thieves use skimming devices on ATMs to capture your card information. Always inspect ATMs for unusual attachments or devices before inserting your card. Cover the keypad when entering your PIN to prevent anyone from seeing it.

Distraction at the ATM: Be cautious of anyone who approaches you at an ATM, especially if they offer help or try to engage you in conversation. Stay focused on your transaction, and if you feel uncomfortable, cancel the transaction and leave.

By adopting these strategies, you can significantly reduce your risk of theft and keep your valuables secure. Remaining vigilant, using anti-theft products, and being aware of common tactics used by thieves will help you navigate public spaces with confidence and protect yourself from opportunistic crimes. Whether you're at home, traveling, or just out for the day, these tips will empower you to stay safer and more secure in any environment.

Safer from Scammers

Scammers employ increasingly sophisticated methods to steal your money, personal information, and even your identity. They exploit various channels, including phone calls, emails, text messages, and online platforms. To protect yourself, it's crucial to stay informed about the latest scams, recognize warning signs, and adopt proactive measures to safeguard your digital and financial security. This guide provides essential tips for identifying and protecting yourself from phone, email, and text scams, securing online purchases, avoiding phishing attempts, and outsmarting common fraudsters.

Identifying and Protecting Yourself from Phone, Email, and Text Scams

Phone, email, and text scams are some of the most common methods scammers use to trick individuals into revealing personal information or sending money. By understanding how these scams operate and knowing what to look out for, you can avoid falling victim.

Phone Scams:

Robocalls and Spoofing: Scammers often use robocalls with pre-recorded messages or caller ID spoofing to impersonate legitimate organizations, such as banks, government agencies, or well-known companies. They may pressure you with urgent language, threatening fines, arrests, or other dire consequences unless you comply immediately.

Recognize Red Flags: Be wary of calls from unknown numbers, especially those claiming to be urgent or demanding immediate action. Legitimate organizations typically do not ask for personal information, such as Social Security numbers, passwords, or bank details, over the phone.

Never Provide Personal Information: If you receive a suspicious call, do not provide any personal information. Instead, hang up and contact the organization directly using a verified phone number from their official website. This ensures you are speaking with a legitimate representative.

Block and Report: Use your phone's built-in features or third-party apps to block unwanted calls and report scam numbers. Many countries have national registries where you can report scam calls, such as the Federal Trade Commission's "Do Not Call" list in the United States.

Email Scams:

Phishing Emails: Phishing emails are designed to look like they come from legitimate sources, such as your bank, a popular retailer, or even a trusted colleague. These emails often contain urgent messages, like account security alerts, requests to confirm information, or offers too good to be true, and typically include links or attachments.

Examine the Sender's Address: Check the sender's email address carefully. Scammers often use addresses that look similar to legitimate ones but have slight variations, such as misspellings or added characters. If something seems off, it's best to ignore the email.

Avoid Clicking Links or Downloading Attachments: Never click on links or download attachments from unknown or suspicious emails. Instead, hover over links to preview the URL and verify if it matches the official website. If you're unsure, visit the website directly by typing the URL into your browser.

Look for Poor Grammar and Spelling: Many scam emails contain noticeable spelling and grammar mistakes, awkward phrasing, or an unprofessional tone. These can be key indicators of a phishing attempt.

Text Message Scams:

Smishing (SMS Phishing): Smishing involves receiving fraudulent text messages that appear to be from a trusted source, such as a bank or government agency. These messages often urge you to click on a link or call a number to resolve an urgent issue, such as confirming a payment or verifying your account.

Verify Before Responding: If you receive a suspicious text, do not click on any links or call the number provided. Instead, contact the company directly using a verified phone number or official website to confirm the legitimacy of the message.

Use Anti-Spam Tools: Many smartphones offer built-in spam filtering tools to block unwanted messages. You can also report spam texts to your carrier, often by forwarding the message to a designated number (such as 7726 in the U.S.).

Tips for Secure Online Purchasing and Avoiding Phishing Attempts

Online shopping is convenient, but it also presents opportunities for scammers to exploit unsuspecting buyers. Following these tips can help you make secure online purchases and avoid phishing attempts.

Shop on Secure Websites:

Look for HTTPS: Before entering any personal or payment information, ensure that the website's URL begins with "https" and includes a padlock icon. These indicate that the site uses encryption to protect your data. Avoid making purchases on websites without these security features.

Use Reputable Retailers: Stick to well-known and reputable retailers when shopping online. Be cautious of unfamiliar websites offering deals that seem too good to be true, as they may be fraudulent. Check customer reviews and verify the legitimacy of the site before making a purchase.

Avoid Public Wi-Fi for Transactions: Public Wi-Fi networks can be vulnerable to hackers. Avoid entering sensitive information, such as credit card numbers or passwords, while connected to public Wi-Fi. Use a virtual private network (VPN) if you need to shop online while away from home.

Protect Your Payment Information:

Use Credit Cards or Secure Payment Services: Credit cards offer more protection against fraud compared to debit cards. Many credit card companies provide zero-liability policies for unauthorized charges. Alternatively, use secure payment services like PayPal, which add an extra layer of protection by keeping your financial information private.

Enable Two-Factor Authentication (2FA): Whenever possible, enable 2FA on your accounts, especially those related to banking or online shopping. This adds an extra step of verification, making it more difficult for scammers to access your accounts even if they obtain your password.

Monitor Your Accounts Regularly: Regularly review your bank and credit card statements for any unauthorized transactions. If you spot suspicious activity, report it immediately to your financial institution.

Avoid Phishing Attempts:

Be Skeptical of Unexpected Requests: Be cautious of unsolicited emails or messages asking you to provide personal information, even if they appear to come from a legitimate source. Companies rarely request sensitive information via email or text.

Educate Yourself on Common Phishing Tactics: Familiarize yourself with common phishing tactics, such as emails that claim your account has been compromised, urgent requests for action, or notifications of unexpected winnings. Understanding these tactics will make it easier to spot scams.

Use Anti-Phishing Tools: Consider installing browser extensions or security software that provides phishing protection. These tools can help identify and block malicious websites, keeping you safe from phishing attempts.

Common Scams and How to Outsmart Fraudsters

Scammers use a wide range of tactics to trick victims. Being aware of common scams and knowing how to outsmart fraudsters can help protect you from financial loss and identity theft.

Impersonation Scams:

Tech Support Scams: In these scams, fraudsters pose as tech support from reputable companies like Microsoft or Apple, claiming there's a problem with your computer that needs immediate fixing. They may request remote access to your computer or payment for unnecessary services.

How to Outsmart: Legitimate companies will not call you unsolicited about computer problems. Hang up immediately if you receive such a call. If you're concerned about your computer's security, contact the company directly using a verified number from their official website.

Lottery and Prize Scams:

The "You've Won" Scam: Scammers notify victims that they've won a large sum of money or a prize but need to pay a fee or provide personal information to claim it. Often, they use well-known names like "Mega Millions" or "Publishers Clearing House" to appear credible.

How to Outsmart: Legitimate lotteries do not require payment to claim prizes. If you didn't enter a contest or lottery, it's a scam. Never send money or share personal details to claim a prize.

Romance Scams:

Online Dating Scams: Scammers create fake profiles on dating sites or social media, building a relationship with their target before inventing a crisis that requires financial help. Victims are often manipulated into sending money or sharing sensitive information.

How to Outsmart: Be cautious when interacting with people you've never met in person. Never send money to someone you haven't met, and be wary of individuals who quickly profess love or avoid meeting in person. Conduct a reverse image search on profile pictures to check if they've been used elsewhere online.

Investment Scams:

Get-Rich-Quick Schemes: Scammers offer investment opportunities with promises of high returns and little risk. These can range from Ponzi schemes to cryptocurrency scams. Often, they use pressure tactics to rush you into making decisions without proper research.

How to Outsmart: Always research investments thoroughly and seek advice from a financial professional. Be skeptical of any opportunity that guarantees high returns with no risk. If it sounds too good to be true, it probably is.

Charity Scams:

Fake Charities: Scammers exploit people's generosity by setting up fake charities, often after natural disasters or during the holiday season. They solicit donations via phone, email, or social media, pocketing the funds instead of supporting the advertised cause.

How to Outsmart: Verify charities through websites like Charity Navigator or GuideStar before donating. Donate directly through the charity's official website rather than through links provided in unsolicited communications.

Rental Scams:

Fake Rental Listings: Scammers post fake rental listings on platforms like Craigslist, asking for upfront payments for deposits or application fees. Once they receive the money, they disappear, and the rental doesn't exist.

How to Outsmart: Always visit the rental property in person before making any payments. Be cautious of landlords who rush you into signing a lease or request payment via untraceable methods, such as wire transfers or prepaid gift cards.

By staying informed, skeptical, and vigilant, you can protect yourself from the ever-evolving tactics of scammers. Implementing these safety measures, recognizing red flags, and knowing how to respond to suspicious requests will help you stay one step ahead of fraudsters and safeguard your personal and financial well-being.

Part 4: Defensive Tools and Techniques

Flashlights: A Tool for Self-Defense

Flashlights are commonly associated with providing light in dark environments, but they can also serve as effective tools for self-defense. Ultra-powerful flashlights, particularly those designed with tactical features, can be used to temporarily blind, disorient, and create escape opportunities during dangerous situations. Choosing the right flashlight and mastering the techniques for using it effectively can enhance your personal safety and provide a non-lethal means of protecting yourself. This guide explores the use of ultra-powerful flashlights for self-defense, techniques for disorienting attackers, and how to select the best flashlight for personal safety.

Using Ultra-Powerful Flashlights for Self-Defense

Ultra-powerful flashlights, often referred to as tactical flashlights, are specifically designed for self-defense and emergency situations. These devices are equipped with high-lumen outputs, sturdy construction, and additional features that make them effective tools for personal safety.

The Basics of Tactical Flashlights:

High Lumen Output: Tactical flashlights are distinguished by their high lumen output, which typically ranges from 500 to over 1,000 lumens. This intense brightness can temporarily blind and disorient an attacker, giving you valuable seconds to escape or respond.

Strobe Mode: Many tactical flashlights feature a strobe mode, which emits a rapid, flashing light. The strobe effect can cause confusion, impair vision, and create disorientation, making it difficult for an attacker to focus on you.

Durability and Design: Tactical flashlights are built to withstand rough conditions. They are typically made from durable materials like aircraft-grade aluminum, making them resistant to impact, water, and extreme temperatures. Many designs also include a serrated or beveled edge around the lens, which can be used for striking in self-defense scenarios.

Compact Size: Most tactical flashlights are compact and lightweight, allowing them to be carried easily in a pocket, bag, or even clipped to a belt. Their small size makes them convenient to have on hand, especially when traveling alone or in unfamiliar areas.

Advantages of Using Flashlights for Self-Defense:

Non-Lethal Option: Unlike other self-defense tools such as pepper spray or tasers, a flashlight is non-lethal and doesn't require special training or permits. It provides a way to defend yourself without causing permanent harm, making it a suitable option for a wide range of situations.

Easy Accessibility: Flashlights are a common, everyday item that can be carried without drawing attention. This makes them an ideal self-defense tool, as they won't raise suspicion when used in public places.

Multipurpose Functionality: Beyond self-defense, a tactical flashlight is a practical tool for everyday use. It provides light in dark environments, can signal for help in emergencies, and can be used to check dark areas around your home or car.

Techniques for Blinding, Disorienting, and Creating Escape Opportunities

To effectively use a flashlight for self-defense, it's essential to understand the techniques for blinding and disorienting an attacker. These methods can provide critical seconds to escape or gain control of a situation.

Blinding and Disorienting an Attacker:

Direct the Beam at the Eyes: The primary method of using a tactical flashlight for self-defense is to direct the beam directly into the eyes of an attacker. The sudden burst of bright light can cause temporary blindness and disorientation, impairing the attacker's vision and ability to focus.

Use Strobe Mode: If your flashlight has a strobe mode, activate it and aim it towards the attacker's face. The rapid flashing light creates confusion and can overwhelm the visual senses, making it difficult for the attacker to concentrate or approach you.

Move While Blinding: While the attacker is disoriented, use this opportunity to move. You can step to the side, back away, or move toward an exit. The goal is to create distance between you and the attacker while they are temporarily incapacitated.

Use Commands: To further disorient the attacker, combine the flashlight's light with verbal commands such as "Stay back!" or "Get away!" Loud, assertive commands can add to the attacker's confusion and reinforce your intent to protect yourself.

Creating Escape Opportunities:

Scan and Move: Use your flashlight to scan your surroundings for potential escape routes. The bright beam can help you identify exits, obstacles, or other individuals who can assist. Keep the beam directed at the attacker as you move to prevent them from recovering and pursuing you.

Use the Environment to Your Advantage: Look for environmental features that can aid your escape, such as stairwells, doors, or other barriers. Your flashlight can help you navigate these areas quickly and safely.

Signal for Help: If you're in a populated area, use your flashlight to signal for help by waving it back and forth or shining it toward potential helpers. The bright light can attract attention and alert others to your situation.

Using the Flashlight as an Impact Tool:

Striking with the Bezel: If the situation escalates and physical contact is unavoidable, use the serrated or beveled bezel of the flashlight as an impact tool. Aim for vulnerable areas such as the eyes, nose, or throat. A well-placed strike can stun the attacker and provide an additional opportunity to escape.

Maintain Control: When using the flashlight as a striking tool, maintain a firm grip and stay balanced. Avoid overextending your arm, which can compromise your stability. Quick, focused strikes are more effective than wide, sweeping motions.

Choosing the Right Flashlight for Personal Safety

Selecting the right flashlight is crucial for ensuring that it meets your needs for both everyday use and self-defense. Consider the following factors when choosing a flashlight for personal safety:

Lumens and Brightness:

Optimal Lumen Range: Look for a flashlight with a lumen range of at least 1,000 lumens. This level of brightness is sufficient to disorient an attacker in most situations. Flashlights with variable brightness settings allow you to adjust the light level according to your needs.

Beam Distance and Focus: A flashlight with a focused beam can reach further distances, making it effective for both self-defense and general use. Some flashlights offer adjustable focus, allowing you to switch between a wide floodlight and a narrow spotlight.

Size and Portability:

Compact and Lightweight: Choose a flashlight that is compact and easy to carry. It should fit comfortably in your hand and be lightweight enough to carry daily without inconvenience. A flashlight that is too large or heavy may be difficult to handle in a stressful situation.

Clip or Lanyard Options: Consider flashlights with clips or lanyard attachments, which provide additional carrying options. A clip allows you to attach the flashlight to your belt or pocket for quick access, while a lanyard can prevent accidental drops.

Durability and Construction:

Material and Build Quality: Opt for flashlights made from durable materials, such as aircraft-grade aluminum, which offer resistance to impact, water, and extreme temperatures. A well-built flashlight will withstand the rigors of everyday use and remain reliable in emergencies.

Water Resistance: Check for water resistance ratings, especially if you plan to use the flashlight outdoors or in wet conditions. Ratings like IPX4 or higher indicate good resistance to water splashes and rain.

Battery Life and Power Source:

Rechargeable vs. Disposable Batteries: Rechargeable flashlights are cost-effective and environmentally friendly, but they require regular charging. Flashlights with disposable batteries offer the convenience of quick replacements but may incur higher long-term costs.

Battery Life: Consider the flashlight's battery life on different brightness settings. A flashlight with a long battery life on medium or high settings is ideal, as it ensures the light will be available when you need it most.

Additional Features:

Strobe Mode: As mentioned, strobe mode is a valuable feature for self-defense, as it can disorient an attacker. Ensure the flashlight you choose includes this mode and that it's easily accessible during use.

One-Touch Operation: In high-stress situations, simplicity is key. A flashlight with one-touch operation or a straightforward control interface allows you to quickly activate the light or strobe mode without fumbling.

Tail Switch: A tail switch (located at the end of the flashlight) provides quick and intuitive access, making it easier to activate in emergencies. Look for flashlights with tail switches that are easy to press, even with gloves on or under stress.

By selecting the right flashlight and learning how to use it effectively, you can add a valuable tool to your self-defense arsenal. A tactical flashlight not only provides a non-lethal means of protecting yourself but also serves as a practical everyday item that enhances your safety in various situations. Whether you're walking home at night, exploring unfamiliar areas, or simply want an added layer of security, a well-chosen flashlight can be a reliable and versatile companion.

Pointed Objects for Self-Defense

In dangerous situations, everyday objects like pens, keys, and other pointed instruments can be used effectively for self-defense. These items are readily available, easy to carry, and can provide a means of protection when other options are not accessible. Knowing how to use these objects correctly can help you deter or disable an attacker, giving you the opportunity to escape. However, it's important to be mindful of legal considerations and safety precautions when using pointed objects for self-defense. This guide covers techniques for using pens, keys, and other pointed items, quick self-defense strategies, and the legal implications of using these tools.

How to Use Pens, Keys, and Other Pointed Instruments for Self-Defense

Pointed objects are not traditionally designed as weapons, but their sharp edges and portability make them practical for self-defense in unexpected situations. Here's how you can use common pointed items to protect yourself:

Pens:

Grip and Position: Hold the pen in a firm overhand grip, similar to how you would hold an ice pick, with your thumb positioned on top to stabilize the pen. This grip allows you to use the pen with maximum force without it slipping from your hand. Position the pen so that the pointed end is facing outward, ready to strike.

Target Vulnerable Areas: Aim for vulnerable areas on the attacker's body, such as the eyes, throat, or face. These areas are sensitive and can cause immediate pain and distraction, giving you a chance to escape. If the attacker's face is not accessible, you can also target soft tissue areas like the armpit or the inside of the arm.

Quick, Repeated Strikes: Use quick, repeated thrusts rather than a single strike. This increases the chance of causing enough pain or damage to deter the attacker. Even a small pen can be highly effective when used with speed and force.

Keys:

Key Between Fingers Method: One common technique involves holding a key between your fingers like a makeshift brass knuckle. However, this method can be risky as it can cause injury to your own hand. Instead, grip the key firmly in your fist with the pointed end sticking out from the bottom of your fist, akin to a small dagger.

Effective Key Strikes: Use a hammer-fist motion to strike with the key, targeting the attacker's face, neck, or other vulnerable areas. The key's pointed edge can puncture skin and cause significant pain, providing an opportunity for you to break free.

Key Flail Method: Another technique involves holding a key ring with multiple keys and using it as a flail. Swing the key ring towards the attacker's face or hands to create a distraction or to inflict pain. The jangling keys can also serve as a noise deterrent, drawing attention to your situation.

Other Pointed Objects:

Comb or Hairpin: Items like a pointed comb, hairpin, or even a small screwdriver can be used similarly to a pen or key. Hold them securely in your hand and aim for the same vulnerable areas. The goal is to cause enough pain to distract or deter the attacker, allowing you to escape.

Using a Screwdriver: A small screwdriver can be especially effective due to its sturdiness and sharp tip. Grip it firmly in an overhand or underhand position and use it to jab at the attacker's body. Focus on sensitive areas like the ribs, throat, or face to maximize the impact.

Quick Techniques to Deter or Disable an Attacker

In a self-defense situation, your primary goal is to create an opportunity to escape. Here are some quick techniques for using pointed objects to deter or disable an attacker:

Focus on Quick, Sharp Movements:

Swift Jabs: The effectiveness of pointed objects lies in their ability to cause pain through quick, sharp jabs. Keep your movements tight and controlled to maintain balance and avoid overextending yourself. Quick jabs to the face or neck can be disorienting and painful, giving you a moment to get away.

Repeated Strikes: Don't rely on a single strike. Use repeated, rapid strikes to overwhelm the attacker. This not only increases the pain inflicted but also reduces the attacker's ability to respond effectively.

Aim for High-Impact Areas:

Eyes and Throat: The eyes and throat are highly vulnerable areas that can incapacitate an attacker quickly. A jab to the eyes can cause temporary blindness or intense pain, while a strike to the throat can disrupt breathing and cause the attacker to recoil.

Soft Tissue Areas: In addition to the face, aim for soft tissue areas that are less protected by muscle or bone, such as the inner arms, under the jawline, or the groin. These areas are sensitive and can cause immediate pain, making them effective targets.

Use Your Voice:

Command and Distract: While using pointed objects, use your voice as a secondary tool. Loudly shouting commands like "Back off!" or "Stop!" can startle the attacker and draw attention from bystanders. A strong verbal response can also reinforce your defensive actions and boost your own confidence.

Draw Attention: Shouting for help or yelling can attract the attention of others nearby. The combination of a loud voice and physical defense with pointed objects can increase your chances of scaring off the attacker or receiving help.

Create Distance:

Move Back Quickly: After delivering a strike, use the momentum to move backward or sideways, creating distance between you and the attacker. Maintaining distance is crucial for avoiding further contact and gives you a clearer path to escape.

Use the Environment: If possible, position yourself with a barrier between you and the attacker, such as a parked car, table, or other obstacles. Use your pointed object to defend while maneuvering towards a safer location.

Legal Considerations and Safety Precautions

Using pointed objects for self-defense carries legal and safety implications that must be considered. Understanding these aspects can help ensure that you use these tools responsibly and within the boundaries of the law.

Understand Local Laws:

Legal Restrictions: Laws regarding the use of objects for self-defense vary by location. Some jurisdictions may consider the use of certain items, like knives or specific pointed tools, as carrying a concealed weapon. Be aware of your local laws to ensure that the items you carry are legal and that you understand the permissible use of force in self-defense situations.

Reasonable Force: In self-defense, the principle of reasonable force applies. This means you can use only the amount of force necessary to protect yourself from harm. Excessive or unnecessary force can lead to legal consequences, even if you were initially defending yourself.

Practice Safety:

Training and Familiarization: Practice using pointed objects in self-defense scenarios to become familiar with their grip, weight, and effective strike techniques. Simple self-defense classes or instructional videos can provide valuable insights and help you build confidence in using these tools.

Self-Injury Prevention: When using pointed objects, there's a risk of self-injury, especially if the item slips or is used improperly. To reduce this risk, practice maintaining a firm grip and using controlled movements. Always be aware of the object's position relative to your own body.

Consider Alternatives:

Other Self-Defense Tools: While pointed objects are useful, consider supplementing them with other self-defense tools such as pepper spray, personal alarms, or self-defense keychains. These items can provide additional layers of protection and may be more effective in certain situations.

Non-Physical Self-Defense: Sometimes, avoiding confrontation altogether is the safest option. Be mindful of your surroundings, trust your instincts, and take proactive steps to avoid potentially dangerous situations whenever possible.

Post-Incident Considerations:

Report the Incident: If you use a pointed object in self-defense, report the incident to law enforcement as soon as it's safe to do so. Provide a clear and honest account of what happened, emphasizing your actions as self-defense.

Seek Legal Advice: In the aftermath of a self-defense incident, consider seeking legal advice, especially if the situation escalated or resulted in significant injury. A legal professional can guide you through the next steps and ensure that your rights are protected.

By understanding how to use pointed objects for self-defense, recognizing the legal considerations, and practicing safe techniques, you can add a valuable layer of protection to your personal safety strategy. Whether you carry a pen, keys, or another pointed tool, being prepared and knowledgeable can make a significant difference in an emergency, empowering you to defend yourself effectively and responsibly.

Chemical Sprays for Self-Defense

Chemical sprays, such as pepper spray and other deterrents, are popular self-defense tools that can effectively incapacitate an attacker, providing a critical window to escape. They are non-lethal, easy to carry, and relatively simple to use, making them a preferred choice for personal protection. However, to maximize their effectiveness and ensure your safety, it's essential to understand how to choose the right product, use it properly, and follow safety protocols for carrying and deploying chemical sprays. This guide explores the effective use of pepper spray and other chemical deterrents, how to select the right product, and key safety tips for handling these tools.

The Effective Use of Pepper Spray and Other Chemical Deterrents

Pepper spray, also known as OC spray (oleoresin capsicum), is the most common type of chemical deterrent used for self-defense. It contains a concentrated form of capsaicin, the active ingredient in chili peppers, which causes intense irritation to the eyes, skin, and respiratory system when sprayed on an attacker.

How Pepper Spray Works:

Immediate Effects: When sprayed directly into an attacker's face, pepper spray causes immediate pain, burning sensations in the eyes, nose, and mouth, difficulty breathing, coughing, and temporary blindness due to the involuntary closing of the eyes. These effects can incapacitate an attacker for 15 to 45 minutes, providing enough time for you to escape.

Range and Coverage: Most pepper sprays have an effective range of 6 to 12 feet, allowing you to maintain a safe distance from the attacker. Sprays are available in different forms, including stream, fog, gel, and foam, each offering varying coverage and wind resistance.

Effective Deployment of Pepper Spray:

Aim for the Face: The key to using pepper spray effectively is accurate aim. Hold the canister with a firm grip and aim directly at the attacker's face, focusing on the eyes. Aiming for the face ensures that the spray makes contact with the most sensitive areas, maximizing the deterrent effect.

Short Bursts: Use short bursts of about 1 to 2 seconds each, rather than a continuous spray. This conserves the product and allows you to reassess the situation after each burst. Repeat as necessary until the attacker is fully incapacitated or retreats.

Create Distance: After spraying, immediately move backward and create as much distance as possible between you and the attacker. The goal is to escape while the attacker is disoriented and in pain.

Be Prepared to Run: Pepper spray provides a temporary defense. It's crucial to use the opportunity to get away quickly and find safety, whether that's moving to a populated area, entering a secure building, or calling for help.

Choosing the Right Product and Proper Usage

With various types of chemical sprays available, choosing the right product can make a significant difference in your ability to defend yourself effectively. Consider the following factors when selecting and using chemical sprays:

Types of Pepper Spray:

Stream: Stream sprays emit a narrow stream of liquid that reaches further distances with greater accuracy. This type is less affected by wind but requires precise aim. Stream sprays are ideal for outdoor use where wind conditions could otherwise disperse the spray.

Fog: Fog sprays release a wider, mist-like cloud that covers a broader area, increasing the likelihood of hitting the target even with less precise aim. However, fog sprays are more susceptible to wind, and there's a higher risk of blowback affecting the user.

Gel: Gel sprays are thicker and stick to the target, reducing the risk of blowback and wind dispersion. They are less likely to contaminate indoor environments, making them a good choice for use in confined spaces such as cars or hallways.

Foam: Foam sprays expand on contact and create a visible barrier on the attacker's face, making it difficult to see or breathe. Like gels, foams are less affected by wind and are suitable for indoor use.

Product Features to Consider:

Safety Mechanism: Look for sprays with a safety mechanism to prevent accidental discharge, such as a flip-top or twist-lock cap. This feature is important for preventing accidental sprays while carrying the product in a bag or pocket.

Ease of Use: Choose a spray that is easy to activate and comfortable to hold. Some models come with ergonomic grips, finger grooves, or keychain attachments for quick access. Test the feel of the canister in your hand to ensure it's easy to handle under stress.

Size and Portability: Pepper sprays come in various sizes, from small keychain models to larger canisters for home use. Consider how and where you plan to carry the spray and choose a size that fits your needs without being cumbersome.

Shelf Life: Check the expiration date of the product, as pepper spray loses its potency over time. Most sprays have a shelf life of about 2 to 4 years. Replace expired sprays to ensure maximum effectiveness.

Proper Usage and Maintenance:

Practice and Familiarize: Familiarize yourself with how the spray works by reading the instructions and practicing with a water-based training spray if available. Knowing how to quickly unlock and deploy the spray can make a crucial difference in a real-life scenario.

Regular Checks: Periodically check the canister for any signs of damage or leaks. Test the spray outdoors occasionally (away from people and animals) to ensure it's still functional and to remind yourself of its range and spray pattern.

Accessibility: Keep the spray easily accessible, such as on a keychain, in an outer pocket, or clipped to your belt. In an emergency, you should be able to access the spray quickly without fumbling.

Safety Tips for Carrying and Deploying Chemical Sprays

While chemical sprays are effective for self-defense, they must be handled with care to ensure your safety and the safety of those around you. Here are some key safety tips for carrying and deploying chemical sprays:

Be Aware of Wind Direction:

Avoid Blowback: When using pepper spray outdoors, always be mindful of the wind direction. Spray with the wind at your back or from the side to avoid blowback that could affect you instead of the attacker. If the wind is strong, consider moving to a position where the wind is less of a factor before deploying the spray.

Legal Considerations:

Know the Laws: Laws regarding the use and carry of pepper spray vary by location. Some areas have restrictions on the size, concentration, or types of sprays that are allowed. Make sure you are familiar with local laws to ensure you are carrying and using the product legally.

Use for Self-Defense Only: Chemical sprays are intended for self-defense and should only be used in situations where you feel threatened or at risk of harm. Misusing pepper spray can result in legal consequences, including charges of assault.

Personal Safety Precautions:

Avoid Exposure to Children and Pets: Keep pepper spray out of reach of children and pets. Accidental exposure can cause severe irritation and distress, requiring medical attention.

Store Properly: Store your pepper spray in a cool, dry place away from direct sunlight and extreme temperatures, which can cause the canister to leak or explode. Do not leave spray canisters in hot cars or places where they can be exposed to heat.

Be Prepared for Self-Exposure: In the event that you are accidentally exposed to pepper spray, remain calm. Avoid rubbing the affected area, as this can worsen the irritation. Rinse your eyes and skin with cold water immediately, and seek medical attention if symptoms persist.

Situational Awareness:

Stay Alert: While carrying pepper spray can enhance your sense of security, it's important not to rely solely on it for protection. Maintain situational awareness, trust your instincts, and take proactive steps to avoid potentially dangerous situations whenever possible.

Have a Backup Plan: Pepper spray is one part of a comprehensive personal safety strategy. Always have a backup plan in case the spray fails or if the situation escalates. This could include retreating to a safe location, calling for help, or using other self-defense techniques.

Dealing with Aftermath:

Report the Incident: If you use pepper spray in self-defense, report the incident to law enforcement as soon as it's safe to do so. Provide a clear account of the situation, emphasizing that your actions were in self-defense.

Seek Legal Guidance: If the use of pepper spray results in significant injury or legal repercussions, consider seeking legal guidance to navigate the aftermath. A legal professional can help you understand your rights and responsibilities.

Chemical sprays like pepper spray offer a practical and effective means of self-defense, especially for those seeking a non-lethal option. By understanding how to choose the right product, use it properly, and follow safety precautions, you can add a valuable tool to your personal safety strategy. Whether you're walking alone at night, traveling, or simply want added peace of mind, carrying a chemical spray can provide the confidence and security you need to protect yourself in uncertain situations.

Conclusion: Living a Safer, Empowered Life

In a world filled with uncertainties, adopting a readiness mentality is essential for personal safety and empowerment. Whether navigating crowded streets, traveling to unfamiliar places, or simply going about your daily routine, being prepared can significantly reduce the risks you face. A readiness mentality involves a proactive approach to personal safety, a commitment to continuous learning, and the practice of essential skills that can help you handle unexpected situations with confidence. This conclusion recaps the key takeaways, encourages ongoing learning and practice, and offers final thoughts on how to live a truly safer and empowered life.

Recap of the Readiness Mentality and Key Takeaways

Throughout this exploration of personal safety, we have highlighted the importance of readiness—a state of being prepared, alert, and equipped to respond effectively to potential threats. The readiness mentality is not about living in fear but about taking charge of your safety and well-being by being proactive rather than reactive. Here are some key takeaways that encapsulate this approach:

Awareness and Vigilance: One of the most important aspects of personal safety is situational awareness. This means being mindful of your surroundings, recognizing potential dangers, and avoiding risky situations whenever possible. By staying vigilant, you can often prevent problems before they escalate.

Practical Self-Defense Tools and Techniques: Equipping yourself with practical self-defense tools, such as pepper spray, flashlights, or even everyday items like pens and keys, can provide a significant advantage in an emergency. Learning how to use these tools effectively, alongside basic self-defense techniques, can empower you to protect yourself and create opportunities to escape from dangerous situations.

Knowledge of Common Threats and How to Counter Them: Understanding common threats, such as scams, theft, or physical confrontations, allows you to recognize warning signs and take appropriate action. Knowledge is power, and by educating yourself about the tactics used by criminals, you can develop strategies to avoid or counteract these threats.

Emphasizing Preparation Over Panic: Preparation is the cornerstone of the readiness mentality. This involves not only having the right tools but also knowing how to use them and having a plan in place. Whether it's having an emergency contact list, knowing the exits in a building, or practicing how to use a self-defense tool, preparation helps reduce panic and enables clear thinking in stressful situations.

Legal and Ethical Considerations: Understanding the legal and ethical aspects of self-defense is crucial. Using force should always be a last resort, and it's important to be aware of your rights and responsibilities when defending yourself. By knowing the laws in your area and choosing appropriate defensive actions, you can protect yourself without unintentionally causing harm or facing legal consequences.

Encouraging Continuous Learning and Practice

Personal safety is not a one-time lesson but an ongoing journey that requires continuous learning and practice. As threats evolve and change, so too must your knowledge and skills. Here are ways to keep your readiness skills sharp and up to date:

Regular Training and Practice: Skills like using self-defense tools, executing defensive moves, or identifying scams require practice to master. Consider taking self-defense classes, participating in workshops, or practicing with friends and family. Regular practice builds muscle memory and confidence, making it more likely that you'll respond effectively in a real-world situation.

Stay Informed About New Threats and Tactics: Criminals are constantly finding new ways to exploit vulnerabilities, whether through technology, social engineering, or physical confrontations. Staying informed about the latest threats can help you adapt your strategies. Follow reputable sources for safety tips, read about recent scams, and stay up to date with current self-defense trends.

Embrace a Learning Mindset: A willingness to learn and adapt is at the heart of the readiness mentality. Approach personal safety as an ongoing education.

Attend seminars, read books, watch instructional videos, and seek out new information that can enhance your understanding and preparedness.

Reflect and Reassess: Regularly reflect on your personal safety strategies and reassess your approach. What worked well in the past may need adjusting as circumstances change. By periodically reviewing your preparedness, you can identify areas for improvement and make necessary updates to your safety plan.

Share Knowledge and Encourage Others: Sharing your knowledge and encouraging others to adopt a readiness mentality can create a safer community. Whether it's teaching a family member how to use a self-defense tool or discussing scam avoidance with friends, spreading awareness can have a positive ripple effect.

Final Thoughts on Living a Truly Safer, Empowered Life

Living a safer, empowered life is about more than just having the right tools or knowing a few self-defense moves. It's a holistic approach that integrates physical preparedness, mental resilience, and a proactive mindset. Here are some final thoughts to inspire you on this journey:

Empowerment Through Preparedness: True empowerment comes from knowing that you have the skills, tools, and mindset to handle whatever challenges may arise. By preparing yourself for potential threats, you're not only protecting your physical safety but also enhancing your confidence and peace of mind. This sense of empowerment extends beyond self-defense; it permeates every aspect of your life, fostering a greater sense of control and autonomy.

Cultivating Confidence, Not Fear: The goal of readiness is not to live in fear but to cultivate confidence. When you're prepared, you can navigate the world with greater assurance, knowing that you have the resources to protect yourself. This confidence is liberating, allowing you to explore new places, meet new people, and engage in new experiences without the constant worry of what could go wrong.

Balancing Caution with Living Fully: While it's important to be cautious and prepared, it's equally important not to let fear dictate your actions. Living a safe and empowered life means finding a balance between being vigilant and fully engaging with the world around you. Embrace the opportunities that come your way, and use your readiness skills as a safety net, not a barrier.

Building Resilience: Resilience is a key component of personal safety. It's the ability to bounce back from adversity, learn from challenges, and continue moving forward. By building resilience, you not only prepare for potential threats but also develop the mental and emotional strength to handle setbacks, recover quickly, and keep pursuing your goals.

Safety as a Community Effort: Remember that personal safety is not solely an individual endeavor. It's a collective effort that benefits from community involvement. Engage with your neighbors, participate in local safety initiatives, and look out for one another. A safer community contributes to a safer individual experience, creating a supportive environment where everyone can thrive.

Embracing a Lifestyle of Readiness: Readiness is more than a set of actions; it's a lifestyle. It's about being mindful, staying informed, and always being one step ahead. By incorporating readiness into your daily routine, you create a foundation of safety that underpins everything you do, allowing you to live with greater freedom and security.

In conclusion, living a safer, empowered life is a journey that combines practical skills, continuous learning, and a proactive mindset. By embracing a readiness mentality, you equip yourself with the tools and knowledge to navigate the world with confidence. Whether it's recognizing a scam, defending yourself from a physical threat, or simply being aware of your surroundings, your commitment to personal safety empowers you to live life on your terms. Keep learning, stay prepared, and remember that the best defense is a well-rounded, well-informed approach to safety. Your journey to empowerment and security is a lifelong pursuit—embrace it with courage and determination.

The Truly Safer Company

Truly Safer coaching empowers people to live happier and freer lives with the confidence that comes from being *truly safer*.

Context-driven Courses

Based on FBI statistics that identify where violent crimes occur, we provide context-driven protocols that provide realistic solutions to avoid and escape from real-world attacks.

Avoidance Strategies

Avoidance strategies teach you to "Think Safe, Be Safe", recognize potential danger, employ avoidance strategies, and manage dangerous confrontations.

Escaping tactics teach you how to use self-defense tools to escape from physical assaults. There is no one-size-fits-all solution to stop attackers, but different tools for different tasks.

For Business

We customize courses to meet the specific needs of your company's personnel at all levels working in a variety of positions and environments.

For Groups

We train private groups, sports teams, entertainers, and high-risk groups potentially targeted for their stance on politics, religion, civil rights, etc.

For People

We train people and families with affluent lifestyles and high-risk profiles like public figures, celebrities, athletes, models, jewelers, influencers, etc.

Training

We offer personal or group sessions, either in-person or virtually, and digital videos to suit your training preferences.

Host a Seminar

For 30+ years, Tom has worked out the easiest way for hosts to have a successful event. Tom provides advertising, hands-on instruction, color certificates, and training tools.

Become a Coach

Become a Coach in our high-quality licensing program that meets professional standards. No previous experience is required; Tom will train you every step of the way.

About Tom Sotis

Tom Sotis has been training consistently in various fighting methods since 1969. In addition to empty hands, weapons, and firearms skills, he is now well recognized as the leading edged weapons instructor in the world recognized for contributions to international and US federal agencies, for his specialized expertise in the use of weapons.

In addition to 50+ years of dedicated training in martial arts, combative methods, tactical knife fighting, and firearms, Tom gained practical street experience through decades of working in conflict-oriented professions.

In the early 1980's Tom began his career in the gang-warfare sections of Los Angeles, California. He was trained as a criminal investigator, undercover investigator, and fugitive recovery agent. Tom returned to New England and operated his own agency, Metro Criminal Investigations, for another ten years.

Tom founded the International Blade Fighters Guild in 1992, dedicated to developing a highly functional method of edged weapons combat, later rebranded as AMOK.

In 1994, Tom was the fourth American to travel deep into Russia became the first American private contractor to train the famed Spetsnaz Counter-Terrorism teams, as well as personnel from the Ministry of Internal Affairs, Russian Criminal Investigation Division Homicide & Major Crimes, and numerous other units. Tom was recognized as an honorary member of the famed Red

Berets, appointed Special Advisor to the Ministry, and honorary Chief Instructor of the CID/HMC division. He returned several times which ultimately became a pivotal point initiating his long career working for US federal agencies.

Tom has since traveled to 25 countries pioneering the forward evolution of edged weapons combat through extensive travel and research. Internationally, Tom's work experience includes, but is not limited to training: Cambodian Special Forces, Danish Law Enforcement, Hellenic (Greek) Coast Guard, Mexican Federal Police and Prison Guards, New Zealand Prison Guards, Norwegian Law Enforcement, South African Military, Police, and Security Forces, and Spanish Law Enforcement.

For over 30 years, Tom has worked with numerous US government agencies, specialist military teams, and various levels of law enforcement agencies. This list includes US Intelligence Agencies, US Special Forces, US Secret Service/ERT, Federal Bureau of Investigation, Drug Enforcement Administration, the Internal Revenue Service, and the New England Organized Crime / Drug Enforcement Task Force.

On the state level, Tom has trained numerous State Police, SWAT, Defensive Tactics Instructors, Municipal Police Departments, County Sheriffs, and Corrections Special Response Teams. While he continues to train Law Enforcement Agencies, Tom serves on the Palm Beach Sheriff's Volunteer Marine Unit.

In the private sector, Tom trains Private Security Firms, Companies and Businesses, Firearms Groups, Combatives Groups, Martial arts organizations, High-risk groups, Community groups, and Individuals.

An avid researcher on psychology and human performance, Tom became a certified Motivation Analyst licensed to administer and interpret the Reiss Motivation Profile®, the world's first scientifically validated and most accurate method of personality profiling and predicting behavior.

Tom Sotis LLC presently comprises three training companies: Truly Safer (Self-Protection), Amok Global (Use of Weapons) and Carry Safer (Defensive Shooting) as well as Performance Optimization Coaching, Motivational Profiling Analysis, and instructional videos on Tactical Knife Fighting, Knife for Self Defense, and Unarmed Knife Defense.

Readers are invited to visit the website

www.TomSotis.com

tom@TomSotis.com

www.ingramcontent.com/pod-product-compliance
Lightning Source LLC
Chambersburg PA
CBHW060521290526
45791CB00001B/484